Using stories to teach ICT

Ages 7-9

Anita Loughrey

Hopscotch
Published by
Hopscotch, a division of MA Education,
St Jude's Church, Dulwich Road,
London, SE24 0PB
www.hopscotchbooks.com
020 7738 5454

©2011 MA Education Ltd

Written by Anita Loughrey

Designed by Claire White,
Fonthill Creative, 01722 717029

Illustrated by Kerry Bailey

ISBN 978 1 90751 5539 2

All rights reserved. This resource is sold subject to the condition that it shall not, by way of trade or otherwise, be lent, hired out or otherwise circulated without the publisher's prior consent in any form of binding or cover other than that in which it is published and without a similar condition, including this condition, being imposed upon the subsequent purchaser.

No part of this publication may be reproduced, stored in a retrieval system, or transmitted, in any form or by any means, electronic, mechanical, photocopying, recording or otherwise, without the prior permission of the publisher, except where photocopying for educational purposes within the school or other educational establishment that has purchased this book is expressly permitted in the text.

Every effort has been made to trace the owners of copyright of material in this book and the publisher apologises for any inadvertent omissions. Any persons claiming copyright for any material should contact the publisher who will be happy to pay the permission fees agreed between them and who will amend the information in this book on any subsequent reprint.

Contents

Introduction..6-7
Curriculum Overview...............................8

School Play – teachers' notes...................9-12
School Play...13-18
Activity sheet 1: Signs..............................19
Activity sheet 2: Plans 20
Activity sheet 3: Poster.............................21
Activity sheet 4: Conflict Resolution............22

Jack and the Beanstalk
– teachers' notes.....................................23-27
Jack and the Beanstalk............................28-35
Activity sheet 1: Jack and the Beanstalk......36
Activity sheet 2: Play Structure..................37
Activity sheet 3: Performance....................38
Activity sheet 4: Evaluating Radio Plays......39

Tiger Adventure – teachers' notes...........40-45
Tiger Adventure.....................................46-51
Activity sheet 1: Database.........................52
Activity sheet 2: Holiday Destinations........53
Activity sheet 3: Branching Database 54
Activity sheet 4: Pie Charts........................55

It's Not Right
– teachers' notes.....................................56-60
It's Not Right..61-63
Activity sheet 1: Local Visit........................64
Activity sheet 2: It's Not Right 65
Activity sheet 3: Letter..............................66
Activity sheet 4: Communication................67

Mosaic – teachers' notes.........................68-71
Mosaic..72-76
Activity sheet 1: Mosaic Design..................77
Activity sheet 2: Repeating Patterns
(Andy Warhol)...78
Activity sheet 3: Symmetrical Patterns........79
Activity sheet 4: Encyclopaedia..................80

Labyrinth
– teachers' notes.....................................81-84
Labyrinth..85-91
Activity sheet 1: Simulations.....................92
Activity sheet 2: Simulation Evaluation.......93
Activity sheet 3: Procedures.......................94
Activity sheet 4: Polygons.........................95
Activity sheet 5: Space Exploration.............96

Using stories to teach ICT Ages 7-9

Introduction

ICT and the Primary Curriculum

Today children will arrive at school with an extensive knowledge of ICT and its capabilities. They have a knowledge and understanding that can sometimes be beyond some adults. The aim in school today is to harness their experiences and use them to enhance their learning in school.

ICT today is one of the best and fastest growing tools available for learning. It helps to:

- Make difficult and abstract concepts easier to explore
- Make learners partners in their formal learning
- Motivate learners and keep them engaged in learning
- Open up dialogue with parents and extend learning
- Personalise learning and give learners a voice
- Raise standards
- Reach the hard-to-reach.
- Save you time and be more efficient.

In order for children to use and apply their ICT knowledge and understanding confidently and competently in their learning and everyday contexts, exciting and stimulating lessons must be provided.

ICT is no longer viewed as a separate curriculum subject but permeates all the other subjects. The children should be provided with stimulating activities that allow them to explore and become familiar with the technology resources available in the school, across a wide range of different subject areas.

About the series

The 'Using Stories to teach ICT' series of books demonstrates how ICT skills can be taught and extended whilst linking to a wide variety of other subject areas. There are four books in the series – two at Key Stage 1 and two at Key Stage 2.

They offer a structured approach with the non-specialist in mind and provide detailed lesson plans to teach specific ICT skills whilst linking to other areas of the curriculum. Each book contains ideas for communication, modelling, presentation, databases and control.

The aim is for ICT to be presented in a format that shows how information technology is used in our everyday lives. The imaginary situations portrayed in the stories act as a stimulus for the children's own investigations and creative work. The ideas in this series can be adapted to teach all areas of the curriculum.

Format of the books

Each book contains six stories that require the children to use and extend different ICT skills. Each story is accompanied by teachers' notes containing four separate lessons that can be used in conjunction with the story. Every lesson plan has a corresponding activity sheet.

The teachers' notes are broken down into the learning objective and the curriculum links with some suggestions for the type of hardware and software that will need to be made available. The activities have been sub-divided into:

- Resources – this is a list of what you will need to do the lesson
- Introduction – ideas to introduce the activities, with key questions and discussion points to reinforce the concepts and vocabulary required for the lesson
- Main activity – ideas for grouping and using the activity sheets
- Plenary – an opportunity to review and discuss the learning outcomes so children reflect on what they have learnt
- Extension – further ideas to extend their skills and technological knowledge.

The activity sheets can be found at the end of each chapter.

About the stories

The stories are designed to be a springboard to develop ICT within the classroom throughout a wide range of subjects due to the broad selection of cross-curricular links.

If possible enlarge copies of the story or project it on to a whiteboard so the children are able to see the illustrations and may be able to follow along as you read it aloud to the class. As the children get older and their vocabulary improves, encourage the children to read the stories aloud to each other.

There is a lot of scope for initiating a discussion about the wide range of technology used in our everyday lives and for extending from the given lesson ideas to your own ICT based projects.

Using the lesson plans

Within the planning we have added reference statements headed WALT, WILF and TIB as these or similar systems are often used to ensure lessons are focused, objective led and in context for the learner. They help summarise the purpose of the lesson, what is required of the children in order for them to successfully learn that lesson and why what they are learning is important.

 WALT stands for "We Are Learning Today"

 WILF stands for "What I'm Looking For"

 TIB stands for "This Is Because"

Curriculum Overview

This chart gives an overview of the ICT covered by each story and the cross-curricular links covered by the activities over all four books in the *Using Story to Teach ICT* series. The relevant information for this book, aged 7-9, is shaded.

Book	Story	ICT	Cross-curricular link
Ages 5-6	Playground Proposal	Modelling	Design & Technology
	Football Crazy	Word Banks	Geography
	Song Quest	Presenting Information	Music
	The Cycle of Life	Labelling and Classifying	Science
	In the Garden	Pictograms	Mathematics
	How Does this Work?	Instructions	Literacy
Ages 6-7	The Pen Friend Diaries	Communicating Information	Literacy
	Celebrations	Communicate Ideas	RE
	Why do we Remember?	Finding Information	History
	Robot Postman	Routes	Geography
	Magic Carpet	Creating Pictures	Art
	Ice-Cream Parlour Break-in	Questions and Answers	Mathematics/Science
Ages 7-9	School Play	Combining Text and Graphics	Literacy
	Jack and the Beanstalk	Manipulating Sound	Music
	Tiger Adventure	Databases	Geography/Mathematics
	It's Not Right!	Email	PSHE/Citizenship
	Mosaic	Repeating Patterns	Art/History
	Labyrinth	Simulations	Mathematics
Ages 9-11	Interior Designer	Graphical Modelling	Art
	Victorian Childhood	Complex Searches	Mathematics /History
	Surprise Party	Spreadsheets	Mathematics
	The Fairground	Control and Monitoring	Design & Technology
	Save the Polar Bear	Monitoring Environment	Literacy
	Security Alert	Multimedia Presentation	Design & Technology

School Play – teachers' notes

Learning Objective
To manipulate text and graphics.

Curriculum Links
Literacy

- Combine words and images to create meaning
- Create and shape their writing, using different techniques to interest the reader
- Select form, content and vocabulary to suit particular purposes.

Activity One – Signs

"Ways of combining text and graphics using Word."

"We need to know how to use words and images together."

Resources
- *Water Babies* by Charles Kingsley
- 'School Play' story
- 'Signs' activity sheet
- Computers
- Printer
- Digital projector
- Whiteboard
- Laptop
- Word.

Introduction

It is a good idea to read the class an adaptation of the *Water Babies* by Charles Kingsley prior to reading the School Play story so the children have some background knowledge of the story that is being referred to.

Read the 'School Play' story to the class. Ask the children what sort of sign did Miss Bennett ask for volunteers to make? Discuss what signs and symbols the children know and are familiar with, such as the boys and girls toilets, no entry signs, wash your hands, no running in the corridors, turn off the lights, close the door, Fire Exit, etc. Talk about where they have seen these signs. Ask the children to describe the signs and explain what they mean. Encourage them to work with a partner and write their ideas on the 'Signs' activity sheet.

Discuss whether signs which use symbols and pictures are easier or harder to understand than a short written instruction. When would a pictorial representation be more useful than a written instruction? Can they think of any signs that would be useful to have in their classroom or around the school? Encourage the children to suggest ideas where specific signs could be displayed in the classroom, or around the school.

Main Activity

Tell the children they are going to make some written signs for around the school and display them. They can use the 'Signs' activity sheet to make a draft plan of their signs and indicate where they would be displayed best. Explain they can produce the signs on the computers using Word.

Show the class the font editing features available in Word, such as changing font style, size and colour. Ask the children to change the look of their signs so it incorporates a wide range of features. Remind the children how to edit text by highlighting words and over-typing them. Allow time for the children to experiment. Explain presentation is important. They should check their spelling and do their neatest work, so that the signs are clear and easy to read.

Remind the children how to save their work and tell them to give their document a name they will easily recognise.

Plenary

Print and display the signs appropriately around the school. Discuss the advantages of using ICT compared to making their signs by hand.

Extension

The children could produce signs on the computer that do not use words but only use pictures to illustrate an instruction, such as: wash your hands, put litter in the bin, quiet in the library, listen, etc.

Using stories to teach ICT Ages 7-9

Activity Two – Plans

"The computer can be used to represent real situations."

"If we move and place objects with accuracy."

"We need to be able to explore options and test our predictions."

Resources
- School Play story
- 'Plans' activity sheet
- Computers
- Printer
- Digital projector
- Whiteboard
- Laptop
- Drawing tool in Word.

Introduction

Read the 'School Play' story to the class. Ask the children what Sophie and Caroline did to create the signs which gave parents directions to the Hall to see their performance of the *Water Babies*.

Use the grid on the 'Plans' activity sheet for children to make a rough draft of where all the classrooms, hall and offices are in the school. They can use this plan to help them when they produce their plans on the computer. Encourage them to add a key to their plans, so they can easily identify all the symbols.

Main Activity

Tell the children they are going to produce an aerial map of the school using the drawing tool in Word, just like Caroline and Sophie.

Demonstrate how to open a new drawing canvas by clicking on the Shapes option on the Insert tab. The New Drawing Canvas option should be at the bottom of the drop-down menu.

A large blue square should appear on the page. Next go into Align on the Drawing tool tab and choose View Gridlines. Also, in the Align dialogue box, you can change the grid settings to alter the horizontal and vertical spacing to 0.5 cms. Now the children can add different sized shapes to the grid to indicate the hall, library area and the different classrooms. At this stage their maps do not need to be to scale.

Allow time for the children to create their plans on the computer.

Plenary

Print out and show their plans. Did they get everything in the right place? Did they miss anything out?

Extension

More able children may be able to using the drawing tool in word to draw the classroom to scale. Explain they need to measure the room, the desks, chairs, etc and work out the sizes accordingly. If they allocate four 0.5 cm squares to a meter they can create a simple scale model of the classroom.

Activity Three – Poster

"To combine text and graphics to communicate meaning."

"If we can recognise the difference between running text and text with line breaks."

"We need to use ICT appropriately to communicate ideas."

Resources
- 'School Play' story
- 'Poster' activity sheet
- Computers
- Printer
- Digital projector
- Whiteboard
- Laptop
- Prepared bank of images connected to the *Water Babies* by Charles Kingsley.

Introduction

Read the 'School Play' story to the class. Discuss with the class how posters are used to give useful information. Where have they seen posters? What sort of information can be shown on a poster? Explain posters are a form of advertising. Ask them to suggest what sort of information would go on a poster advertising a school play. Ask the children to work with a partner and list their ideas on the 'Poster' activity sheet. Encourage them to share these ideas with the class and list their contributions on the whiteboard.

Discuss the use of different techniques that could be used on the poster, such as:

- Alliteration
- Bright colours
- Pictures
- Powerful words
- Questions
- Repetition
- Rhyme
- Short, snappy sentences.

Talk about the possible audience for a poster advertising a school play. Where could the poster be located? What age group might the poster be aimed at? How would this affect the content and layout? Discuss the type of lettering they might use on a poster. How could they produce this lettering so it is big enough to read from a distance? Tell them they could use stencils or they could use WordArt and increase the font size. Demonstrate how to change styles and increase the font size using WordArt.

Main Activity

Tell the children they are going to design a poster for the *Water Babies* play, or if there is a performance or event coming up shortly within the school they could design a poster to advertise this instead.

Explain they will be making their posters on the computer. They can add WordArt and pictures, ClipArt and their own photos to the posters to make them more visually appealing.

Use the 'Poster' activity sheet to draw a rough design of how they want their poster to look. Ensure they have included all the important information such as day, time, place, etc. Ask them to consider whether it is visually appealing and if it can be read easily to find the information required.

Allow time for the children to produce their posters on the computer. Encourage them to select and insert appropriate pictures from a prepared bank of images using copy and paste. Remind them to use key word searches when locating images in a large database. Show the class how to re-size a graphic so that it fits on the page.

Children should also choose font styles, colour and size appropriate to the size of paper they will be using to print them out. Remind the class how to edit text using WordArt. Encourage them to use Print Preview to check their posters. Ensure words are not cut off in the middle and continued on the next line. Explain this would the poster difficult to read.

Plenary

Print and display the posters around the school. Show the class some examples of the posters produced, using a whiteboard and a data projector. Ask the children to explain their choices of font size, colour and layout. What have they learnt? What might they do differently next time?

Extension

Discuss how adverts not only inform but, persuade people to do things. Encourage the children to consider what sort of sentences they could use to persuade people to come to the performance of the *Water Babies*. Ask them to list these persuasive words and phrases, such as fantastic performance, wonderful, buy your tickets now, don't miss out, once in a lifetime opportunity, etc.

Activity Four – Conflict Resolution

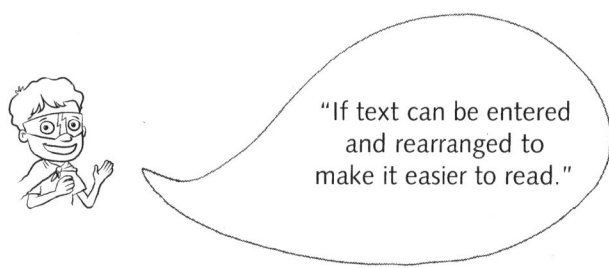

"If text can be entered and rearranged to make it easier to read."

Resources

- 'School Play' story
- 'Conflict Resolution' activity sheet
- Computers
- Printer
- Digital projector
- Whiteboard
- Laptop.

Introduction

Read the 'School Play' story to the class. Why did Brendon and Robin fall out? Were they good friends before? Do you think Brendon was being unreasonable when he said that Robin could not use the photographs? Why? Do you think Robin was being unreasonable not letting his friend win the competition? Why? What would you have done in this situation?

Scan the 'Conflict Resolution' activity sheet into the computer and project onto the whiteboard. Explain to the children the first illustration shows a picture of Robin and Brendon fighting over the camera and the second illustration shows them shaking hands, making friends again.

Main Activity

Split the class into pairs. Give each pair a copy of the 'Conflict Resolution' activity sheet. Ask the children to discuss what might be being said. Encourage the children to role play a discussion between Robin and Brendon to show how they made up their differences.

The children should then either:

- use a word processor to type the speech, print it and stick it onto photocopies of the activity sheet;
- load the 'Conflict Resolution' activity sheet into a drawing program software such as Paint and ask the children to type directly into the speech bubbles.

Ask the children to save their work and print a copy.

Plenary

Ask for volunteers to share their role plays and show what they have written in the speech bubbles on the 'Conflict Resolution' activity sheet.

Extension

Ask the children to draw pictures and write their own speech bubbles of what Robin and Brendon might say if they never managed to make up their differences, explaining why each of them think they are in the right and the other person is being unreasonable. This could be done using a drawing program such as Paint.

School Play

I sat in the hall with my housemaid costume on, watching the dress rehearsal for the end of year play. It was an adaptation of the *Water Babies* by Charles Kingsley and we had been practising for weeks.

"Don't make me climb the chimney today," Robin said, keeping in role as Tom, the chimney sweep. He gave a deep, hoarse cough, just like Miss Bennett had told him to do, to show his lungs had been damaged by the soot.

Brendon shoved him. He was playing Grimes, the mean old man that forced Tom to climb the chimneys. "You'll do as you're told," he growled. "Get up that chimney." Brendon shoved Robin again.

Robin stumbled backward just like they'd practiced.

Miss Bennett clapped. "Well done everyone. That was marvellous."

"That went well," Brendon said to Robin. Robin smiled. "Yeah, it was fun."

"Now everyone, I want you to listen carefully. We are going to have a competition to see who can design the best programme cover to hand out to the parents when they come to watch the play."

"A competition? Cool!" Brendon shouted out. I put my hand up.

"Yes Caroline," Miss Bennett said.

"What's the prize?" I asked.

"Good question Caroline," Miss Bennett smiled. "The prize is family tickets to see the pantomime at the local theatre."

Using stories to teach ICT *Ages 7-9*

There was a wave of whispers.

"We should enter that," I whispered to my best friend Sophie, who sat next to me wearing her water baby costume.

She nodded.

"I also need volunteers to make some signs to direct people to the Hall to watch the play," Miss Bennett said.

Another wave of whispers echoed around the room. But, nobody volunteered.

"You can use the computer room to make the signs," she said.

Brendon nudged Robin. Robin looked at him and groaned. "Me and Brendon will do it Miss," Brendon yelled.

Sophie did that thing where she looked at me and expected me to know what she is on about. She kept raising her eyebrows and jolting her head in the direction of Miss Bennett.

"What?" I whispered.

"Is that it? Only two volunteers," Miss Bennett said.

"We'll do it too." Sophie waved her arm in the air.

"Thank you," Miss Bennett said.

The bell went for lunch. We changed out of our costumes and rushed to the computer room. Brendon and Robin were already there. They had not bothered getting changed.

"We've started making our programme cover designs for the competition." Robin said. Both of their designs had a massive heading saying *Water Babies* in WordArt. They were taking photos of themselves to add.

"But, they're going to look exactly the same," Sophie said.

"We've used different font and colours in our headings," said Robin.

"And I can use the photos and Robin will do something else," said Brendon.

"I thought we were going to share the photos," Robin said.

"No way! I want to win this competition." Brendon laughed. "My little brother loves pantomimes."

Robin snatched the camera from him. "That's not fair."

"Give that back," Brendon shouted.

"Why? It's not yours!"

"It's not yours either. It belongs to the school."

They were tugging at the camera, just as Mr Western, the Headteacher, walked into the computer room. "What are you two doing?" He marched towards them and took the camera away.

"Go straight to my office now," he ordered, pointing at the door.

Brendon and Robin left. Mr Western glared at us.

"We're making signs for Miss Bennett," I mumbled and he left, slamming the door behind him.

* * *

Sophie and I decided to make the signs using WordArt and we even made a map of the school using the drawing tool in Word. But, we did not have time to start our programme covers before we had to go and have our lunch.

Using stories to teach **ICT** *Ages 7-9*

***

The next day at rehearsals it was obvious Brendon and Robin still had not made up after their fight with the camera. They were both on stage.

"Don't make me climb the chimney today," Robin said.

There was a long pause. Brendon stared angrily at him.

"Don't make me climb the chimney today," Robin said louder.
"You forgot to cough," Brendon said with his hands on his hips.

Robin clenched his fists. "Don't make me climb the chimney today." Robin coughed loudly.

"You'll do as you're told. Get up that chimney." Brendon pushed Robin really hard towards the cardboard chimney.

He fell backward and landed on his bottom. He glared up at Brendon. "You did that on purpose," he yelled and leapt to his feet.

I jumped up onto the stage and stood between them. "Come on you two," I said. "It's not worth it." I stared into Robin's eyes and he started to relax. He counted slowly under his breath.

"What are you doing Caroline? The housemaid is not in this bit," Miss Bennett said. "OK, since you're there, let's take it from the part where the housemaid thinks Tom has stolen something from the big house. Places everyone and…. Action!"

"Thief, thief," I yelled, pointing at Robin.

Robin ran across the stage in the direction of Grimes.

"What have you been up to boy? Have you been stealing?" Brendon grabbed Robin's wrist.

"Ouch, you're hurting me." Robin snatched his hand away. There was a red mark on his wrist where Brendon had grabbed him. "Watch it!" Robin's fists were clenched again. "Just say your line, will you?" Brendon turned his back on Robin and walked to the front of the stage. "Miss Bennett, Robin is ruining the play."

Miss Bennett sighed. "OK you two, concentrate on delivering your lines. Nice and loud so we can hear them from the back. Brendon, try not to be so rough. Remember you're acting! You shouldn't be hurting people for real. Try that bit again."

They both took their places.

"Thief, thief!" I yelled again, pointing at Robin.

"What have you been up to boy? Have you been stealing?" Brendon went to grab Robin's wrist.

Robin jumped back quick. "No. I haven't. I wouldn't," he said.

Brendon tried to grab him again and Robin kept leaping out of the way. The rest of the class started to giggle.

Miss Bennett clapped her hands loudly. "What's the matter with the two of you today?"

Everyone stopped what they were doing and looked at her.

"Remember we've not got long now. The performance to the rest of the school and to your parents is only next week. Also, I have good news about the pantomime. The local theatre has agreed to give us enough tickets for the whole of Year Six to go and watch it."

Everyone cheered.

I put my hand up.

"Yes Caroline," Miss Bennett said.

"What about the Programme cover?" I asked.

Miss Bennett smiled. "I think I will take a photo of all of you in your costumes and use it as the cover design. For some unknown reason, Mr Western handed me the school camera this morning and that gave me the idea. Now, we'll have the water babies on stage while Brendon and Robin take five minutes to sort out their differences."

Using stories to teach **ICT** *Ages 7-9*

I jumped off the stage and Sophie climbed on. A few minutes later, I glanced over at Brendon and Robin. They were shaking hands and smiling. I was so pleased they had made up. Now everything could get back to normal.

The End

Signs

Name: _____

- Write down and draw some of the signs and symbols you know.

```
┌─────────────────────────────────────────────────────┐
│                                                     │
│                                                     │
│                                                     │
│                                                     │
│                                                     │
└─────────────────────────────────────────────────────┘
```

- Design your own sign to use in the classroom

```
┌─────────────────────────────────────────────────────┐
│                                                     │
│                                                     │
│                                                     │
│                                                     │
│                                                     │
└─────────────────────────────────────────────────────┘
```

- Where would your sign best be displayed?

_____
_____
_____

Using stories to teach **ICT** *Ages 7-9*

Plans

Name: _____

- Draw an aerial plan of your classroom on the grid below.

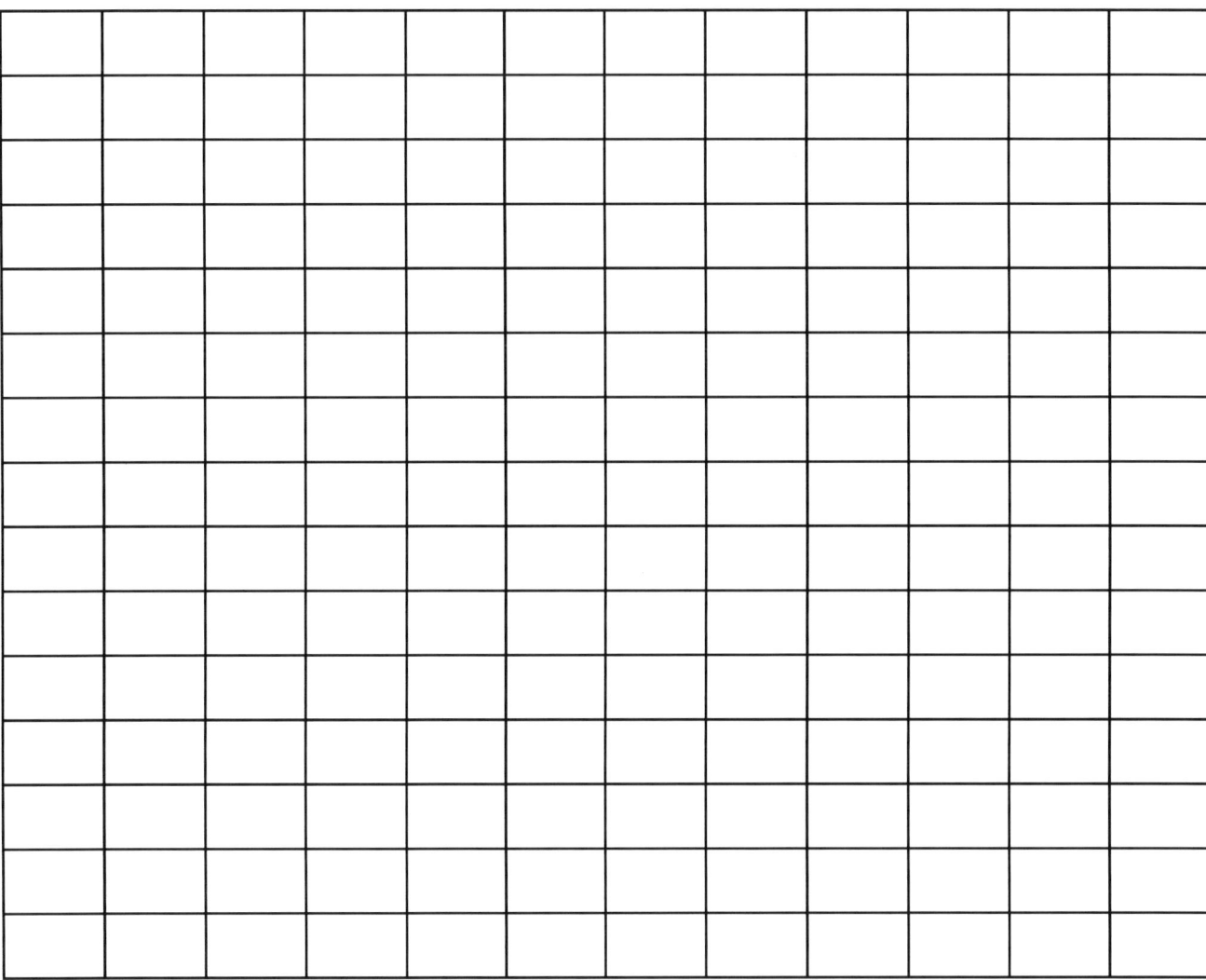

- Draw a key to show what all your symbols mean.

Poster

Name: _____

- What information would go on a poster?

  _____
  _____
  _____

- Design your own poster for the Water Babies play.

```
┌──────────────────────────────────────────────┐
│                                              │
│                                              │
│                                              │
│                                              │
│                                              │
│                                              │
│                                              │
│                                              │
│                                              │
└──────────────────────────────────────────────┘
```

- Re-produce your poster on the computer.

Using stories to teach **ICT** *Ages 7-9*

Conflict Resolution

Name: _____

- Write what Robin and Brendon are saying in the speech bubbles.

Jack and the Beanstalk – teachers' notes

Learning Objective
To manipulate sound and music

Curriculum Links
Music

- Compose and choreograph a collective audio performance and record it
- Improvise, rehearse, refine and use ICT to improve their performances
- Listen carefully, recognise and use sound effects.

Activity One – Performance

"Explore and develop musical ideas using ICT."

"If we can use ICT to record sounds."

Resources
- 'Jack and the Beanstalk' radio play
- 'Jack and the Beanstalk' activity sheet
- Computers
- Digital projector
- Whiteboard
- Laptop
- Audio recorders
- Windows sound recorder
- Electronic keyboards with a range of sounds and the ability to store and play sequences
- Other percussion, string and wind instruments
- Digital microphone.

Introduction

Read the radio play, 'Jack and the Beanstalk' to the class. Discuss the differences between a radio and a stage play. Explain how the radio can not use visual clues like a stage play can. They can not see people on the radio everything must be done through sound to let the audience know who everyone is. Explain this could be done by using different music and sound effects to show who is on the stage, their mood and actions. This means they need to think very carefully about the sound effects they will need and how they might produce the desired effect.

Discuss some of the different techniques they could use such as:

- CD musical accompaniment
- Use of musical instruments
- Build from soft and slow to quick and frantic
- Changing their voices
- Clapping
- Door slamming
- Stamping /running feet
- Tapping
- Whispering
- Silence.

Explain electronic keyboards can be used to select and control sounds. They can also experiment with music software to create simple melodies that could represent the different characters.

Main Activity

Tell the children they are going to record the 'Jack and the Beanstalk' radio play in small groups. Split the class into groups of six children.

Explain before they start that they need to plan what they are going to do. Tell them to write down on the 'Jack and the Beanstalk' activity sheet, the name of the child who will read each character. Then they should read through their parts together and list the sound effects needed and how they might make these sound effects.

Allow time for the children to experiment with different sound effects and note their choices on the 'Jack and the Beanstalk' activity sheet. When they are ready they should record their versions of Jack and the Beanstalk. This can be done with audio recorders, or using the windows sound recorder on the computer and digital microphones. Explain they must follow the scripts carefully so they know when each particular sound effect is to be used and to ensure they do not miss their cue.

Plenary

When the groups have recorded their radio play ask the children to listen to each others and analyse the different sound effect techniques and methods they have used. Discuss the differences between the live and the electronically-controlled sound effects they used.

Extension

Experiment with use of voice. Ask the children to record a sentence in monotone. Then record the sentence again using a different intonation, such as a question or exclamation. Listen back to the impact of the change.

Explain meaning can change depending on which words are emphasised, such as:

- **I** want to see the play
- I **want** to see the play
- I want **to** see the play
- I want to **see** the play
- I want to see **the** play

Record the different versions and discuss how the meaning changes.

Activity Two – Structure

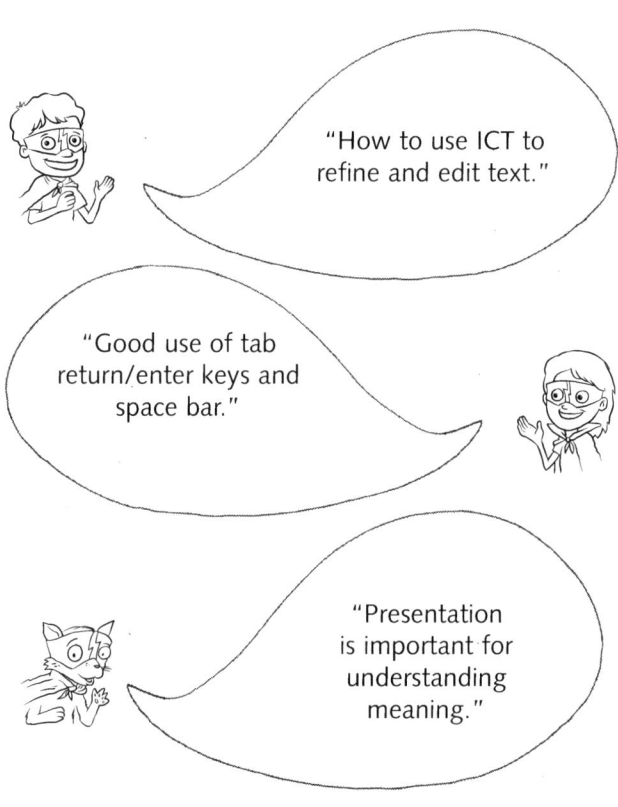

"How to use ICT to refine and edit text."

"Good use of tab return/enter keys and space bar."

"Presentation is important for understanding meaning."

Resources
- 'Jack and the Beanstalk' radio play
- 'Play Structure' activity sheet
- Computers
- Printer
- Digital projector
- Whiteboard
- Laptop.

Introduction

Scan the play into the computer and display using the digital projector. Discuss the way it is laid out and the presentation of the play. Explain to the class plays have a specific format when they are written. Point out how each character is easily identified because the name of who is speaking is written on the left hand side and what they say is on the right hand side. Point out the sound directions are written in brackets.

Allocate the parts to six children and have them read the 'Jack and the Beanstalk' radio play to the class. Tell them to pay particular attention to how the playwright has indicated the play should be read. Point out the emotional reactions, such as: pleased, puzzled, scared, angry, etc.) Explain these words indicate to the actors how the character should sound.

Tell the children they are going to investigate the structure of the play. Ask the children how many acts are there? Are the acts divided into scenes? What is the length of the play? How many characters are there? What are the ages and gender of the characters? Did the playwright provide any indication of the characters' personality?

Split the class into small groups and ask them to complete the 'Play Structure' activity sheet. Explain that analysing plays will help them to write their own.

Main Activity

Tell the children that they are going to write their own radio plays based well known fairy tales such as Cinderella, Snow White, Three Little Pigs, etc. Split the class into groups of six children.

Tell them they should use the observations they wrote down on the 'Play Structure' activity sheet to write their own play based on a well known fairy tale. They should remember to use the correct layout and to provide the cast with instructions on how the characters should be acted. Tell them there should be a beginning (Act 1), middle (Act 2) and an end (Act 3). They should decide what part of the story should be included in each act. Tell them not to worry about the sound effects at this point, but they should keep in mind that it is a play that will be listened to rather than acted on a stage.

Encourage them to write their plays straight onto the computer taking turns to have a go at the keyboard. Reinforce that all the children should contribute with ideas for the dialogue. Demonstrate how to use the tab key to leave a space between the characters' name and what they are saying. Show them how to use the backspace key to take the cursor back to the margin. Point out they should hold the shift key down at the same time as they press the bracket keys, in just the same way as they would make a capital letter.

Show them how words in a sentence can be changed without deleting the whole sentence. Remind them to save their work at regular intervals.

When they have written the play on the computer they can go through it as a group and decide where to put the sound effects. These can be added to their plays. Remind them they should read the play through as a group to make sure it flows well and they have not missed anything out.

Plenary

Discuss the advantages and disadvantages of using ICT to draft and redraft the script as opposed to writing ideas out by hand. Make two columns on the whiteboard. Are there more advantages, or more disadvantages?

Extension

Some groups could print out their play and swap with another group. Each group could try a preliminary reading of the play and note down any parts they did not understand or ideas that could improve the plays. The groups can then make amendments accordingly.

Activity Three – Performance

Resources
- 'Jack and the Beanstalk' radio play
- 'Performance' activity sheet
- Own scripts of well known fairy tales from previous lesson
- Computers
- Printer

Using stories to teach **ICT** *Ages 7-9*

- Digital projector
- Whiteboard
- Laptop
- Audio recorders
- Windows sound recorder
- Electronic keyboards with a range of sounds and the ability to store and play sequences
- Other percussion, string and wind instruments.

Introduction

Play a few of the previously recorded Jack and the Beanstalk plays to the class. Ask the children to remind you how they produced the sound effects to help tell the story. What did they find difficult? What did they find easy?

Tell the children they are going to record their own radio plays using the scripts they wrote previously. Give each group a copy of the Performance activity sheet. Tell them to write down a list of their characters and who will play each character. Explain they should go through their play carefully and list the sound effects they need. How are they going to source the sound effects?

Remind them they can use their voices to produce sound effects and they can add different intonation to what the characters say to add meaning. They can also use the electronic keyboards and music software to create their own appropriate compositions.

Main Activity

Allow time for the children to experiment with different sound effects and note their choices on the Performance activity sheet.

When they are ready they should record their versions of their fairy tale. This can be done with audio recorders, or using the Windows sound recorder on the computer. It is a good idea to provide somewhere quiet where the children are able to do this. This may mean staggering the use of the computer room and music facilities.

Plenary

The children should listen to their recordings to make sure that their voices are clear and the story makes sense.

Extension

Discuss what changes they would need to make to their plays if they were going to perform them on stage.

Activity Four – Evaluating Radio Plays

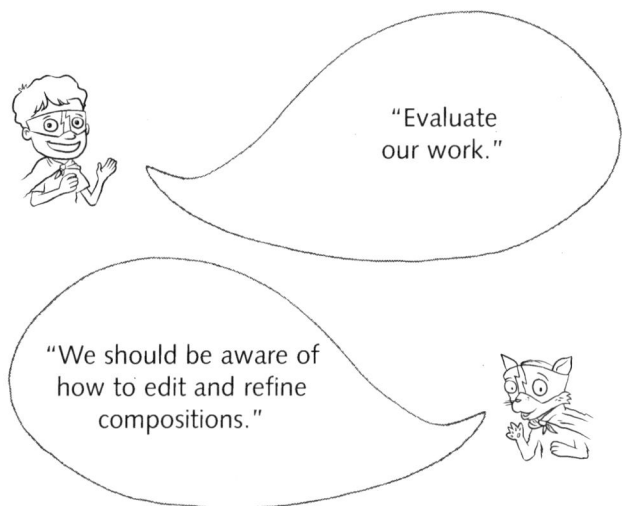

Resources
- 'Jack and the Beanstalk' radio play
- 'Evaluating Radio Plays' activity sheet
- Computers
- Printer
- Digital projector
- Whiteboard
- Laptop.

Introduction

Split the class into different small groups. Allocate each group one of the fairy tale recordings. It does not matter if it is their own play or not. Ask the children to listen to the play in their group. Explain to the class they are going to evaluate the plays. They should think about what worked well and how could they make them better.

If possible, provide each child with headphones to listen to the play so that they concentrate on the recording and do not talk through it.

Main Activity

Give each group a copy of the 'Evaluating Radio Plays' activity sheet. Tell them they are going to analyse the different sound effect techniques and methods that were used in the recording they are listening to. Is there any part of the play where it is not clear what is happening? How could they make it clearer?

Each group should allocate a scribe to write down their ideas. If desired they could write on A1 paper rather than on the activity sheet itself and use the sheet to refer to the questions. Encourage the children to note down good and bad examples from the radio plays they are listening to.

Plenary

When they have finished each group should play the recording and present their opinions to the rest of the class. Do the others agree? Why or why not?

Extension

The children could give the recordings of their plays to other classes in the school to listen to and enjoy. Discuss which classes their plays would be more suited to. Encourage them to consider the age and abilities of their audience.

Jack and the Beanstalk

Characters:

Mum	Old man
Jack	Mrs Giant
Cow/Hen	Giant

Act One - Scene One

(Music to show Mum and Jack entering.)

Mum: Where's that lazy boy? Jack! Jack! Where are you?

Jack: Yes, Mum. **(Yawns.)** What do you want?

Mum: Where have you been?

Jack: I was busy sleeping under the apple tree.

Mum: There's no time for sleeping. I need you to go to market and sell Clara, our cow.

Cow: Mooooo.

Mum: We need money to buy food.

Jack: O.K, Mum.

Act One – Scene Two

(Music. Sound of Clara and Jack walking to market.)

Old man: Hello, Jack. Where are you going with that old cow?

Cow: Mooooo.

Jack: I'm going to sell her at the market. We need money to buy food.

Old man: The market is such a long way away, why don't you sell her to me? I'll take good care of her.

Jack: How much money will you give me?

Old man: I haven't got any money but I've got these beans. **(Sound of magic beans rattling.)** They're magic beans.

Jack: Magic beans! **(Excited.)** And I won't have to walk all the way to market. O.K! It's a deal.

Cow: Mooooo.

(Sound of Jack swapping Clara for the beans. Music for Jack returning home.)

Act Two – Scene One

(Music to indicate Mum is there.)

Mum: Back so soon. Did you manage to sell Clara?

Jack: **(Sounds very pleased with himself.)** Yes, I certainly did.

Mum: Well done, Son. How much did you get for the old cow?

Jack: You'll never guess.

Mum: Ten pounds.

Jack: Nope. **(Sound to indicate Jack shaking his head.)**

Mum: Twenty pounds.

Jack: Nope. **(Sound to indicate Jack shaking his head.)**

Mum: Thirty pounds.

Jack: I told you, you'd never guess. I didn't get money. I got these beans.

(Sound of Jack shaking the bag of magic beans.)

Mum: **(Sounds puzzled.)** Beans? You sold our only possession for a bag of beans?

Jack: They're magic beans.

Mum: **(Sounds angry.)** Magic beans. **(Noise of snatching bag out of Jack's hand.)** I don't believe it. You stupid boy. How could you sell Clara, for … **(Sound of the beans falling out of bag.)** … beans?

(Angry music. Footsteps of Mum stomping away and slamming the door.)

Jack: Some people don't appreciate anything. I think I will have a snooze under the apple tree. That walk has completely worn me out.

Act Two – Scene Two

(Jack yawns. Music to show beanstalk growing. Music to show Mum is back.)

Mum: Wake up Jack. Where did this massive big beanstalk come from?

Jack: **(Yawning.)** It must have been those beans. See, I told you they were magic. It goes right up through the clouds.

Mum: What use is a beanstalk to us? It doesn't even have any beans on it. It blocks out the light and will stop all the other plants from growing. Get an axe and chop it down.

Jack: O.K, Mum.

(Sound of Mum leaving. Sound of Jack fetching an axe.)

Jack: It's a bit hot for chopping down beanstalks. **(Sound of dropping axe.)** I'll do it later when the sun goes down. I wonder how tall it is. I'm going to climb it and find out. Maybe I'll find some money to buy food at the top.

(Music for Jack climbing beanstalk.)

Jack: Phew! It's even hotter up here. This is thirsty work. **(Sound of Jack stopping for a rest.)** Wow! You can see for miles. There's a castle high up on those clouds. I'm going to find out who lives there. Maybe, I could get a nice cool drink and something to eat.

(Music to show Jack has finished climbing the beanstalk.)

Act Three - Scene One

(Sound of Jack walking to castle and knocking on the door. Door creaks open. Music to show it is Mrs Giant opening the door.)

Using stories to teach **ICT** *Ages 7-9*

Mrs Giant: **(Surprised.)** This is no place for a young lad. My husband's a mean, fierce giant and he eats little boys like you on toast.

Jack: Please, could I have something to drink? I've been climbing for ages and I'm really thirsty. A refreshing, cold glass of water would be great. Oh, and that toast sounds good too.

Mrs Giant: You're taking a terrible risk. My husband will be home any minute. He'll be tired and very, very hungry.

(Sound of heavy footsteps approaching.)

Mrs Giant: **(Scared.)** Quick that's him now. Hide. Get in the cupboard.

(Jack runs into cupboard.)

Mrs Giant: Wait until he's asleep. He always falls asleep after he's eaten.

(Mrs Giant closes the cupboards door. Enter Giant.)

Giant: Fee-fi-fo-fum
I smell the blood of an Englishman,
Be he alive, or be he dead,
I'll grind his bones to make my bread.

Mrs Giant: That must be the lovely sauce I've made. I used the scraps of the little boy you had for yesterday's dinner.

(Hear chair scrape on floor and Giant sits down.)

Giant: Bring me my food, woman?

Mrs Giant: Here it is. **(Sound of plates being put on the table.)**
And here's the sauce I was telling you about.

(Giant eats noisily.)

Giant: Wife. Bring me the hen that lays the golden eggs!

Mrs Giant: Yes, dear.

(Hen music. Sound of hen clucking.)

Giant: Lay!

(Sound of hen laying a golden egg. Sound of hen clucking.)

Giant: A beautiful golden egg.

(Jack gasps.)

Giant: Did you hear something?

Mrs Giant: Must have been the poor hen. You've already got more golden eggs than you know what to do with.

Giant: Get out of here.

(Sound of plate flying across the room and smashing.)

Mrs Giant: I'm going to bed. **(Music to show Mrs Giant is leaving.)**

Using stories to teach **ICT** *Ages 7-9*

Giant: Lay!

(**Sound of hen laying another golden egg. Sound of hen clucking. Giant falls asleep at the kitchen table, snoring loudly. Jack creeps out cupboard.**)

Jack: A hen that lays golden eggs. That's just what we need at home. We'd never be hungry again.

(**Music for Jack grabbing the hen and running away.**)

Hen: Help! Help! (**Sound of hen clucking.**)
Jack: Sssh!
Hen: Help! Help! (**Sound of hen clucking.**)

(**Sound of yawning as Giant wakes up.**)

Giant: Where are you going with my hen? Come back here you scrawny boy. (**Music to show the Giant is chasing Jack. Music to show that Jack climbs down beanstalk.**) Come back here. (**Sound of Giant stamping his feet at top of beanstalk.**)

Act Three – Scene Two

(Music and sound of Jack chopping down the beanstalk. Music to show Mum entering.)

Mum: Haven't you chopped that beanstalk down yet? I asked you to do it hours ago. Busy sleeping under the apple tree, I suppose. You're such a lazy boy. **(Sound of hen clucking.)** And where did this hen come from?

(Beanstalk comes down with a crash.)

Mum: Be careful boy! Are you trying to kill me? That beanstalk nearly landed on my head.

Jack: **(Panting.)** But, Mum look! I've got a magic hen.

Mum: Magic hen?

Jack: Yes, watch. Lay.

(Sound of hen laying a golden egg. Sound of hen clucking.)

Mum: A golden egg! You'd never believe it, a magic hen. Our money worries are over. Well done, Son. **(Happy music.)** We'll never be hungry again.

The End

Jack and the Beanstalk

Name: _____

- Who will play each character?

Mum _____

Jack _____

Cow/Hen _____

Old man _____

Mrs Giant _____

Giant _____

- Read the play together and note down what sound effects are needed.

_____
_____
_____
_____

- How will you make these sound effects?

_____
_____
_____
_____

Play Structure

Name: _____

- Look at the Jack and the Beanstalk play and answer the following questions:

1. How many acts are there? _____

2. Are the acts divided into scenes? _____

3. How many scenes are there? _____

4. How long is the play? _____

5. How many characters are there? _____

6. How old are the characters? _____

7. Are they male, or female? _____

8. How did the playwright provide an indication of personality?
   _____
   _____
   _____

9. List some of the characters' emotional reactions:
   _____
   _____
   _____

Performance

Name: _____

- List your characters and who will play them.

Character	Who will play them

- What sound effects are needed and how will you make them?

Sound effect needed	How to make the sound effect

Evaluating Radio Plays

Name: _____

- Listen to the radio play and answer the following questions.

1. Could you identify when all the characters were coming on or leaving the stage? Give an example.

   _____
   _____
   _____
   _____

2. How did the sound effects show the characters' personalities?

   _____
   _____
   _____
   _____

3. Were there any parts where you could not understand what was happening? Why were they difficult to understand?

   _____
   _____
   _____
   _____

4. Are there any sound effects you would have added or taken out?

   _____
   _____
   _____

Tiger Adventure – teachers' notes

Learning Objective
To make sense of data in an increasingly digital world

Curriculum Links
Geography

- To know where significant places are located in the UK, Europe and the wider world
- To identify similarities and differences between places and environments, and understand how they are linked
- To recognise different parts of the world have different weather and climate.

Mathematics

- To generate and explore questions that require the collection and analysis of information
- To enter information into a database and use the database to answer simple questions
- To create pie charts and branching databases to find out the answers to specific questions.

Database programs such as Black Cat Information Workshop 2000 can be used by the children to produce their own simple databases. It is important before starting these activities that you have set up the fields in the database to match the database activity sheet. This will save time and frustration. Consider number, text and choice of fields. Black Cat Information Workshop 2000 is particularly good as they can produce graphs from their data in the same software package. The choices of graphical representations include horizontal and vertical bar charts, pie charts, line and scatter graphs, which can be manipulated and shown in 2 or 3 dimensions.

Activity One – Database

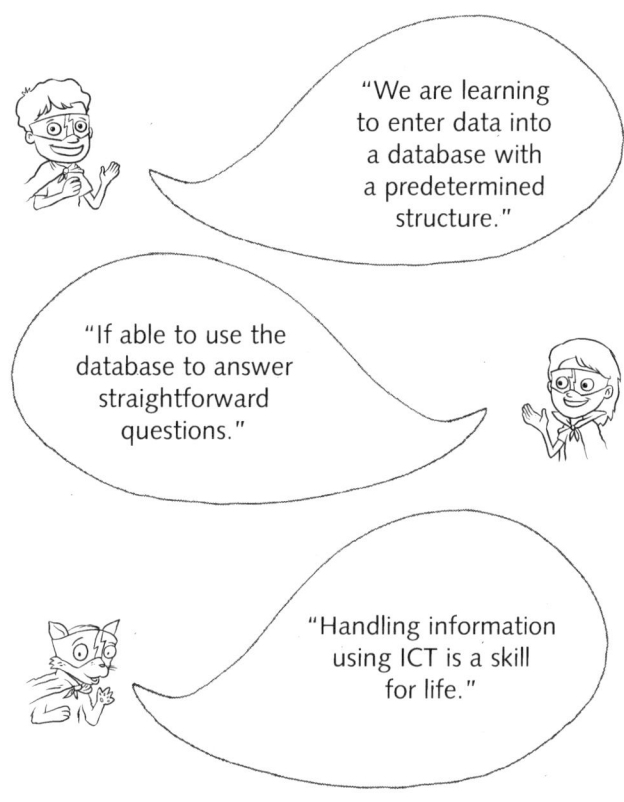

"We are learning to enter data into a database with a predetermined structure."

"If able to use the database to answer straightforward questions."

"Handling information using ICT is a skill for life."

Resources
- 'Tiger Adventure' story
- 'Database' activity sheet
- Data projector
- Laptop
- Computers
- Globes
- Atlases
- A selection of travel brochures and leaflets
- Online world maps
- Search engine
- Satellite image program, such as Google Earth (or similar)
- Database program, such as Black Cat Information Workshop 2000.

Introduction

Read the story, 'Tiger Adventure' to the class. Where is the rainforest where the tiger lives? What do they know about India? How can they find out more about this country?

Look at online maps and programs like Google Earth to find out where India is. Show the children on a globe where about it is in relation to the UK. Remind the children how they can find a specific place by doing a search for it in an online search engine. Point out in what climatic zone India is compared to the UK.

Allow them time to explore globes, atlases and a selection of travel brochures and leaflets. Ask them where they would like to go on holiday. What would their ideal holiday destination be?

Main Activity

Tell the children they are going to find out more information about their favourite holiday destination. They can use the Internet, atlases, globes and travel brochures. Ask the children to find out what continent their favourite holiday destination is in. What climate zone is it in? What is the population of the country? What is the main holiday activity they can do at this destination, e.g. sunbathing, fishing, skiing, swimming, hiking, dancing, etc. What essential items would they need to take with them, e.g. walking boots, sun block, warm clothes, sleeping bag, etc. Encourage them to think of their own questions to answer about their favourite holiday destination.

Ask them to fill in the form on the 'Database' activity sheet, with the information they found out. Explain that the 'Database' activity sheet has been structured to contain the same fields as the computerised database. Discuss how it is difficult to find information when it is not organised. Tell them having the same fields will help them to find the information more quickly.

Demonstrate how to add a record to a database using your own 'Database' activity sheet that you have previously completed. Split the class into pairs and ask the children to enter the information from their 'Database' activity sheets into the database. Ensure each child has added their information to the database and that it has been added into the correct field.

Plenary

When each group have entered their information come back together as a class and ask the children to suggest a question they can ask the database, such as:

- Which country has the largest population?
- How many favourite holiday destinations are in Europe?
- Where could I go fishing?
- What is the most popular climate for a holiday destination?

Discuss the advantages and disadvantages for using the computer to do this, compared to using the 'Database' activity sheet to find out the information.

Extension

Discuss what it means if there is no answer. Give an example where this will happen. Does this mean they are wrong? Does this mean the database is broken? Remind them that the computer has had to go through the whole file, counting how many records match each category.

Explain that a database can only work with the information it has been given. If there is not an answer it means that the database does not have the necessary information and more data may be needed to be collected.

Activity Two – Holiday Destinations

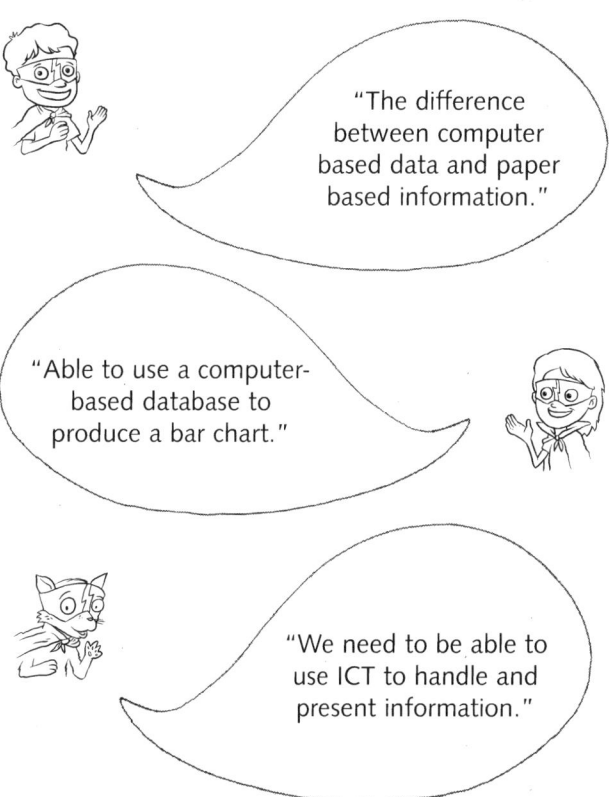

"The difference between computer based data and paper based information."

"Able to use a computer-based database to produce a bar chart."

"We need to be able to use ICT to handle and present information."

Resources

- 'Tiger Adventure' story
- 'Holiday Destinations' activity sheet
- Previously completed Database activity sheet
- Data projector
- Laptop
- Computers
- Globes
- Atlases
- A selection of travel brochures and leaflets
- Online world maps
- Search engine
- Satellite image program, such as Google Earth (or similar)
- Database containing information on favourite holiday destinations previously entered.

Introduction

Read the story, 'Tiger Adventure' to the class. Tell the children Jane wanted to go to India to see the tigers. Ask the children what favourite holiday destinations did they choose when they completed the 'Database' activity sheet. Tell them they are going to collect this data in the form of a tally to show their favourite holiday destination.

Demonstrate how to make a tally of favourite holiday destinations on the whiteboard. Ask the children to copy this tally and convert the data into a simple bar chart using the 'Holiday Destinations' activity sheet.

Main Activity

Ask the children if they can think of an easier way to produce graphs. Remind them they have already input the information about their favourite holiday destinations into the computer. Use the database to demonstrate how they can produce bar charts.

Divide the children into groups and ask the children to produce bar charts for other things, such as population, how many countries are in each continent, most popular holiday activity and most essential items to take. Encourage them to use the bar charts to ask questions such as: Which country has the largest population? Which country has the smallest population? Etc.

Ask the children to write a few sentences to explain what their graph shows. Ask them to write down three questions to ask other children about the graph.

Plenary

Discuss the advantages of using ICT to draw graphs, compared to when they drew them by hand on the 'Holiday Destination' activity sheet. Which was quicker? Tell the children computers have the advantage of speed and accuracy.

Extension

Ask the children to plot where the favourite holiday destinations for the whole class are on a world map. They could add the country's flags using an image search engine.

Activity Three – Branching Database

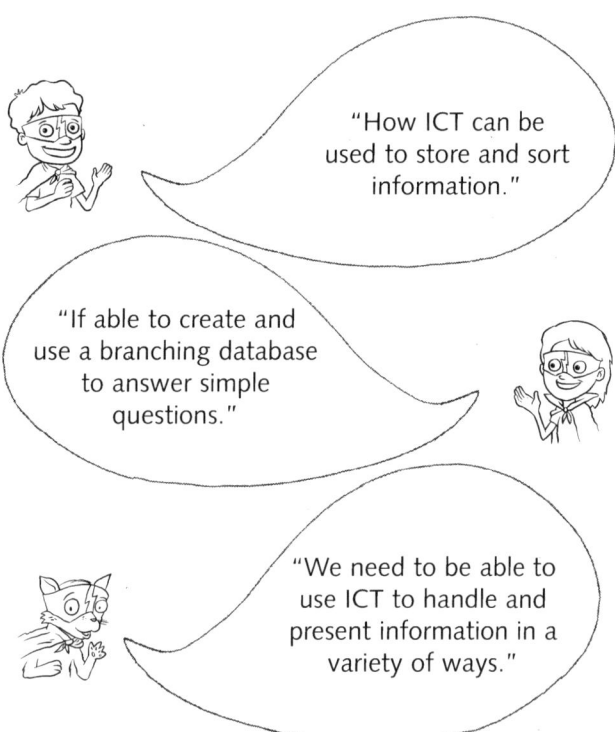

"How ICT can be used to store and sort information."

"If able to create and use a branching database to answer simple questions."

"We need to be able to use ICT to handle and present information in a variety of ways."

Resources

- 'Tiger Adventure' story
- 'Branching Database' activity sheet
- Computers
- Printer
- Digital projector
- Whiteboard
- Laptop

- A selection of travel brochures and leaflets
- Branching database program such as Decisions 3 or Flexitree 2.

Decisions 3 is a simple to use branching database in which information can be entered in the form of a 'decision tree'. The program has been designed to be as easy to use as possible and is recommended for children from the age of six years upwards. Flexitree 2 is a similar program that enables the user to create and edit branching data bases. With Flexitree 2 it is also possible to view the whole 'decision tree'.

Introduction

Read the story, 'Tiger Adventure' to the class. Ask what questions Jane's mum asked her customers. Point out these are, yes/no questions.

Tell the children a branching database is a way of classifying a group of objects and identifying a specific person, or item by asking a series of 'yes' or 'no' questions. Explain you can narrow down the types of holiday destinations people would like to go to, by asking a series of questions likes Jane's mum did at the Travel Agency.

Remind the children of the need to ask yes/no questions and ask them to suggest what sort of questions might be asked. Make a list of their ideas on the whiteboard. For example:

- Do they like to go somewhere hot?
- Is it in Europe?
- Do they want a swimming pool?
- Is it important to have a restaurant?
- Is it near the equator?
- Do they have want to stay in a tent?
- Are they looking for adventure?

Show the children the 'Branching Database' activity sheet. Demonstrate using the tree diagram on the branching database activity sheet. Explain this is one possible way of sorting information using some of the questions the children identified. Tell them they can use different questions to sort holiday preferences in other ways as well.

Main Activity

Choose a selection of the most popular holiday activities from those identified by the children in their holiday destination database. Split the class into small groups of three or four children. Ask them to think of yes/no questions to identify these different activities and write them onto the Branching database activity sheet. Ask each group to test the others' database.

Remind the children how to input their questions into the software available to produce a branching Database, which other people can also use to answer questions about their favourite holiday activity. Allow time for them to input their information and test their databases.

Plenary

Reinforce that a branching database can be used to classify and sort a wide range of things, such as fruit and vegetables, musical instruments, vehicles, materials, shapes, numbers, etc. Explain they can also use all their senses to help sort things such as sounds, smell, taste and how things feel to touch.

Extension

The children can extend their skills and practice using a wide variety of branching databases online, using websites such as, www.mape.org.uk.

Using stories to teach **ICT** *Ages 7-9*

Activity Four – Pie Chart

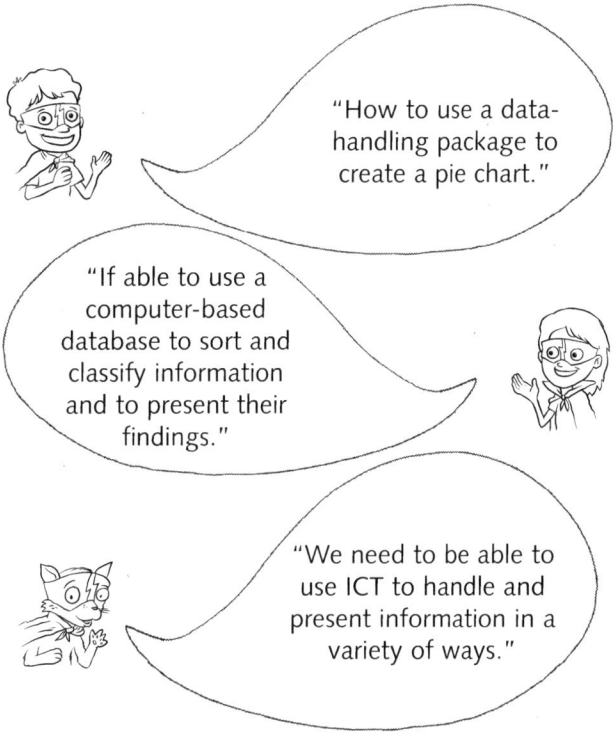

"How to use a data-handling package to create a pie chart."

"If able to use a computer-based database to sort and classify information and to present their findings."

"We need to be able to use ICT to handle and present information in a variety of ways."

Resources
- 'Tiger Adventure' story
- 'Pie Chart' activity sheet
- Completed holiday destinations database
- Black Cat Information Workshop 2000
- Computers
- Printer
- Digital projector
- Whiteboard
- Laptop
- Graphic program or Word
- Selection of holiday brochures and leaflets.

Introduction

Read the 'Tiger Adventure' story to the class. Ask would they like to go and see the tigers in India? Remind them India is a country and it is in the continent Asia. What other continents do they know?

Remind the children how they collected data about their favourite holiday destinations using the 'Database' activity sheet. Tell them this was a standardised sheet, which made it easier to enter and check the information. Point out it was also easier because the structure of the sheet matched the fields. Remind the class about number, text and choice of fields. Remind the class the computer will only treat things the same if they are called the same thing.

Tell the children they are going to use a simple graphing program to make comparisons. Explain that most pie charts can be used to make comparisons. Tell the children this is another way of representing data and makes it easier to recognise quantities and see differences at a glance. Explain ICT is an excellent medium for creating pie charts.

Main Activity

Split the class into pairs. Talk about the software program Blackcat Information Workshop 2000 or other software they may be using and answer any questions. Remind the children about taking turns. Explain one person can input the data while the other checks that the data is correct and then they can swap roles.

Find the saved holiday destination database. Use the information to produce pie charts. Suggest the children label the sections and give their pie chart a title. Encourage them to check they have got the numbers correct and have not missed any out.

The pie chart can be produced using the Chart facility in Word, if no other software is available in school. Ask the children to print out their pie charts and stick them onto the 'Pie Chart' activity sheet. Ask them to think of three questions they can answer by looking at the information shown by the pie chart. Tell them to write these questions on the 'Pie Chart' activity sheet. This is easier to do when they are printed out or you could display them side by side on the whiteboard with a data projector.

Plenary

Compare the pie charts to the bar charts they produced on the 'Holiday Destinations' activity sheet.

Explain they show the same information. Which one do they find easier to understand?

Discuss the advantages of using ICT to produce graphs and charts. Explain to the children it is easier to see the information at a glance, questions can be answered more easily and it can be quicker.

Extension

Ask the children what is a travel brochure. What sort of information does it contain? What is the difference between a leaflet and a brochure? Tell them a leaflet is normally one sheet of paper whereas, a brochure is like a glossy magazine.

Discuss with the class how travel brochures and leaflets are used to give useful information. Where have they seen travel brochures? What sort of information is shown? Explain travel brochures and leaflets are a form of advertising. Ask them to suggest what sort of information would go on a leaflet advertising their favourite holiday destination. Explain a lot of the information they collected for their database would be very useful for tourists.

Ask the children to make their own travel leaflets, using their data and graphs to persuade people to go there. The leaflets could be printed and stapled together to produce a class book of favourite holiday destinations.

Tiger Adventure

Jane was bored. She picked up a travel brochure from the shelf. It said Explore India on the front cover. She sat on the floor of the travel agency, where her Mum worked, and flicked through the pages. She had to come to work with her Mum today as the babysitter had phoned in sick.

"Would you like to go somewhere hot?" her Mum asked the little old lady with the walking stick sat at her desk.

Jane gazed at a picture of the Indian rainforest. In the photograph she could see a tiger in the undergrowth partially camouflaged by leaves. Opposite was a photograph of three cute tiger cubs.

"Mum, where's India?" she shouted.

"Have a look at the map," her Mum said.

Jane groaned as she got up from the carpet and went to look at the massive map of the world pinned to the wall behind her Mum's desk.

"A week in Cornwall would be ideal," the little old lady said and Jane's Mum typed the lady's details into the computer.

Jane found India on the map. It was in Asia. She was surprised at how big the country was compared to the United Kingdom. She went back to the brochure she had left lying on the floor.

"Do you want a swimming pool?" Her Mum asked the couple holding hands, now sat in front of her.

Jane flicked back a few pages. She jumped up. "Here's a nice picture of a swimming pool," she yelled. "Would you like to go there?" She waved the brochure at the couple.

"Jane go and sit down and don't interrupt," her Mum said. "I'm trying to work." Her Mum glared at her. Jane went and sat back down on the carpet.

"Don't sit there, Jane," her Mum said. "You're in the way. Go sit at the little table." Her Mum pointed at the tiny red plastic table with two little blue chairs, only really suitable for a three-year-old, right at the back of the shop. There was some paper and crayons in the middle of the table.

Jane sat on one of the tiny blue chairs and started to copy the picture of a tiger cub from the Explore India travel brochure.

"What are you drawing?" a voice asked.

Jane spun around, no one was there. Her Mum was busy with another customer.

"Do you want to go skiing?" she heard her Mum ask.

"Up here," the voice said.

Jane looked up. All she could see was a dusty, brown teddy bear sat on top of a filing cabinet. It was wearing a blue knitted jumper with a yellow sun on it.

"That's right. It's me," the teddy bear said. Jane's eyes widened. "You talked."

"Don't be so surprised," said the bear.

"Who are you?"

"I'm Bertie the travel agency mascot. What are you drawing?"

"A tiger," Jane replied.

"If you get me down off here I will take you to see a real tiger," Bertie said.

Jane took one of the blue plastic chairs over to the filing cabinet and stood on it. She picked Bertie up and brushed some of the dust off him. She sat Bertie on the table next to her drawing.

"Close your eyes and hold on to my paws," Bertie said.

Jane did as she told. There was a sudden breeze that swept her hair into her face. When she opened her eyes she was standing with Bertie in the middle of a beautiful, green rainforest.

BANG!!!

Jane jumped. "That sounded like a gun shot."

"Did you get it?" she heard a man yell.

There was lots of shouting and she could hear people running though the foliage toward them.

"Quick," Bertie said. "We must hide." He zipped through the rainforest and Jane followed.

"What is it?" she asked, gasping for breath. Large ever-green leaves slammed against her legs and arms.

"Poachers," Bertie replied. "Keep running!"

There was a rustling noise in the thick green bushes near-by. Jane could feel her blood pumping. She wasn't going to get away in time. She glanced behind her and saw a little tiger cub pushing its way out through the branches.

Thinking quick, Jane dashed back and snatched the cub from the ground. She couldn't let this little cub get caught by the poachers. Holding the cub under her arm she darted through the rainforest until they could not hear the men's voices anymore.

"They must have gone in the other direction," Bertie said.

Jane put the little cub down. "Where's your Mum?" she asked.

The cub stared up at her with big golden eyes. She knew its mother must have been caught by the poachers.

"We have to go save her," Jane said.

"How can we?" Bertie said. "A ten-year old girl and a teddy bear against grown men, we don't stand a chance."

"But, we can't just do nothing! This cub won't survive without its Mum," Jane said. "Oh, OK," Bertie said reluctantly.

They doubled back in a wide circle until they found the poachers' camp. There were several big cages and tents. Most of the cages were empty but, in the one furthest away was a tiger, pacing up and down. The cub ran straight to the cage and started to paw between the bars. The mother tiger leant through the shiny metal bars and licked her cub. Next to her, in a smaller cage were two more cubs that looked exactly the same as the one they had found.

"But, how are we going to get them out?" Jane asked.

"We need to look for a key."

Jane went into one of the tents. There was a radio system on the desk and a bunch of keys. She grabbed the keys.

"Oi, what are you doing here?" a gruff voice came from behind her.

She froze.

"What are you doing with those keys?" A big-bellied poacher walked slowly towards her. Two more poachers arrived and were stood in the doorway of the tent, blocking Jane's way out.

"Look what I just found outside the tiger's cage," a tall, skinny poacher said. "It's a teddy bear."

The other men laughed.

"Lost your teddy bear, have you little girl," the big-bellied poacher jeered. "Well, I think we've got a cage big enough for the both of you."

"I wonder how much money we would get for a little girl," the bald poacher with a ring through his nose said.

"Ouch!" the tall, skinny poacher yelled. "The teddy just bit me."

He dropped Bertie on the ground. Bertie grabbed him around the ankle and the poacher fell to the floor with a thump.

Jane was not going to hang around to be captured. She ran out of the tent with the keys and unlocked the mother tiger's cage.

"Hey, you can't do that," the bald poacher with a ring through his nose yelled.

The mother tiger pushed open the unlocked cage door and growled at the poachers.

The poachers huddled together. Jane undid the cage of the cubs and they leapt for joy on their brother they were so pleased to be back together again. The mother tiger kept growling at the poachers and circled around them. They backed away.

Soon the tiger was standing between them and the tent. The poachers edged backward towards the cages. The cubs crouched on the ground and looked like they were going to leap on the three mean men. Bertie ran out of the tent straight towards them. Jane did not know who they were more scared of Bertie or the tigers. They turned and ran into the cage. Jane slammed the cage door shut quick and locked it.

Then she rushed back to the tent and used the radio to call the authorities. They said they would be there soon. The mother tiger and her cubs disappeared into the rainforest. Jane was glad she had united the mother tiger with her cubs and trapped the poachers. But, she was not going to wait around for the authorities to get there.

"It's time we were getting back," she said.

She held onto Bertie's paws and shut her eyes. The wind swirled around her and when she opened her eyes again she was back at the travel agency.

"Jane are you ready to go home." Mum got up from behind her desk and walked over to where she was stood by the red plastic table. "Wow! What a beautiful drawing of a tiger. It's so life-like. You've been such a good girl today. I hardly knew you were here. Well done."

Jane looked up at Bertie who was sat back on the filing cabinet. He winked at her and she smiled.

The End

Database

Name: _____

- What is your favourite holiday destination?

_____

- Use the Internet to find out more about your favourite holiday destination.
- Complete the form below:

Country	
Continent	
Climatic zone	
Population	
Main holiday activity	
Essential item	
How to travel there	

Holiday destinations

Name: _____

- Create a tally chart to show the favourite holiday destinations in your class.

Favourite holiday destination	Tally	Total

- Use the information to make a block graph.

7									
6									
5									
4									
3									
2									
1									

- What does your graph show?

_____

Branching Database

Name: _____

- Use the branching database to find your partner's favourite holiday destination.

Pie Charts

Name: _____

- Use the information you collected about the favourite holiday destinations in your class to create a pie chart.
- Print and stick your pie chart below.

```
┌─────────────────────────────────────────────────────────┐
│                                                         │
│                                                         │
│                                                         │
│                                                         │
│                                                         │
│                                                         │
│                                                         │
└─────────────────────────────────────────────────────────┘
```

- Think of three questions that you can answer using your pie chart.

1 _____

2 _____

3 _____

Using stories to teach **ICT** *Ages 7-9*

It's Not Right! – teachers' notes

Learning Objective
To create and respond to emails and attachments to gather information and communicate with others

Curriculum Links
PSHE/Citizenship

- Undertake investigations and enquiries
- Understand how and why places and environments develop and how they may change in the future
- Present and communicate findings, develop arguments and explanations using appropriate specialist vocabulary and techniques, showing sensitivity to the needs of an audience.

One of the underlying aims of these activities is for the children to understand how and why places and environments develop and how they may change in the future by undertaking an investigation. In order to do this, the children are expected to find things that need improving about an area near to where they live and formulate their own persuasive argument on why action is needed to improve it.

To get the most out of this collection of place activities, you will need to identify a local location suitable for improvement to take the children on a visit. This can include points of praise for other areas in comparison.

Activity One – Local Visit

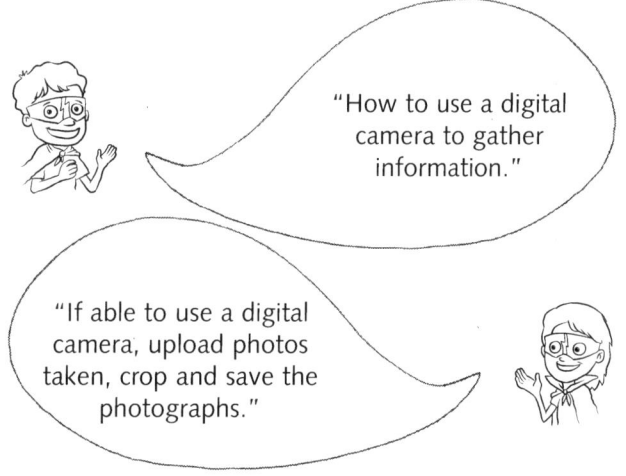

Resources
- 'It's Not Right!' letter
- 'Local Visit' activity sheet
- Digital cameras
- Data Projector
- Laptop
- Computers.

Introduction

Read the letter, 'It's Not Right!' to the class. Ask the children why was Josie upset? Ask the children, what areas of 'natural beauty' have they visited? What did they like about them? Would they be upset if the area was vandalised and dirty? Why?

Organise a visit to a public environmental area of natural beauty, such as a local park area, or local public garden, canal or river path, lake, etc. So the children can investigate the area first hand.

Remember to get parental permission before you take the children off site.

On the visit ask the children to list good and bad things about the area. Take photos as evidence. Use the 'Local Visit' activity sheet to focus the children's attention. If you want you could visit two areas, one that you feel has excellent facilities, and another that requires improvement. Encourage the children to notice the facilities available such as fences, paths, dustbins for litter and dog waste, benches, etc. Ask the children why it is important to have these things. Ask the children if they have been kept in good condition. Look for evidence of vandalism.

Split the class into small groups of three or four children and let them take pictures of particular features in the area that could be improved, using a digital camera. In contrast, they could take pictures of things they like as examples of how they would like things improved. Explain the pictures they take are going to be used back in the classroom.

Main Activity

Demonstrate to the children how to upload and save a photograph on the computer, using the software available. Discuss why they should save their photos as jpegs or gif files. Tell them that these types of documents are more likely to be recognised by photographic software that may be different to what they use in school.

In their small groups of approximately four children ask them to upload the photographs they took on their park visit and save them each with a distinct name that they will remember.

Demonstrate how to reduce the size of their photographs. Ask them to reduce the size of one of their photographs and save it with a different file name, using the 'Save as' function. Demonstrate how to crop their photos to make the focus of the picture more central. Allow time for the children to practice cropping and saving their photos.

Plenary

Ask each group to choose their favourite photo and show the 'before' and 'after' shots to the class. Ask:

- What do they like about it?
- How could they make it better?

Extension

The children could print and write a few sentences in Word about their favourite photo for a display in the classroom of their recent visit.

Activity Two – It's Not Right!

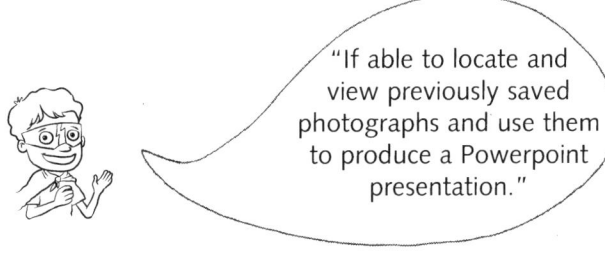

"If able to locate and view previously saved photographs and use them to produce a Powerpoint presentation."

Resources

- 'It's Not Right!' letter
- 'It's Not Right!' activity sheet
- Computers
- Printer
- Digital projector
- Whiteboard
- Laptop
- Satellite image program, such as Google Earth (or similar)
- Microsoft PowerPoint or other multimedia presentation package.

Introduction

Read the letter, 'It's Not Right!' to the class. Ask the children did they find similar problems when they were on their visit? Tell the children they are going to use the evidence they collected to make a PowerPoint presentation to explain the problems to their own local newspaper, county council or their MP and what things could be done about them.

Ask the children to find the file in which they uploaded their photographs from the visit. The children should be able to open the file and view their photographs. Check that everyone is able to do this.

Explain they will be using their notes and photographs from their visit as evidence and examples to support their key points. Split the class into pairs to record their ideas with their partner on the 'It's Not Right!' activity sheet. They can use the photos to help jog their memory of the visit.

Tell the children they will need to select a style and vocabulary appropriate to their audience. Remind the children the audience in this case is their local newspaper, county council or their MP. Find out who your local MP is and some information about them and their policies. Or, find a named person to write to on the council or at the newspaper.

Discuss the techniques they will need to use in presenting and linking points persuasively and suggesting ways forward. Explain there should be a statement indicating their point of view, some background information on the issue, facts with evidence to support them and a conclusion with their suggestions at the end of the presentation.

Main Activity

Allow the children to work with a partner. Tell them to use the notes they made on the 'It's Not Right!' activity sheet to make a PowerPoint presentation of their persuasive argument.

It may be necessary to limit the amount of slides to about six to eight. The children should sequence their photos in line with their persuasive argument. Encourage the children to give opinions on what they saw and add sentences to their presentations to provide more information.

Ensure they save their presentations regularly, as they will need them again for a future lesson.

Plenary

Let each group show their presentation to the class or a school assembly. Provide opportunities for their peers to comment on the PowerPoint presentations. Ask:

- What did they like best about the presentation?
- How could they make the presentation better?

Extension

If time permits allow the children time to improve their presentations, especially if you plan to send one of them to your local newspaper, county council or MP.

Activity Three – Letter

Resources

- 'It's Not Right!' letter
- 'Letter' activity sheet
- Computers
- Printer
- Digital projector
- Whiteboard
- Laptop.

Introduction

Read the 'It's Not Right!' letter to the class. Split the class into pairs. Tell the children they are going to write their own letters about the area they have visited to email to their local newspaper, county council or MP. Decide on which option you prefer before you start the lesson.

Allow time for them to plan and compose their letters on the 'Letter' activity sheet before typing them up in Word. Encourage them to sequence their points in order to present a logical and persuasive argument on why the local area needs improvement. They can use the notes they made on the previous activity sheets to help them. Encourage the children to be careful over spelling, punctuation and clarity. Stress to the children that they are writing letters to an important person in authority and they want to create a good impression.

Main Activity

Tell the children they are going to type up the letters they have written on the activity sheet, in Word. Allow time for them to organise and reorganise their text on screen. Demonstrate how to use features like the spell check to help them edit their work. Explain they still have to check their writing after using the spell check because sometimes it may insert the wrong word, as it does not recognise mistakes where a real word is used, such as using 'there' instead of 'their', or 'them' instead of 'then', or 'if' instead of 'it'. It is important that they read back what they have written. The spell check is an aid rather than a substitute.

Explain to the class they can change font size and use bold to make some ideas stand out as more important than others. Tell the children that it is not good practice to use all capitals in emails. This is considered as shouting, which is rude and so must be avoided. Explain they can use cut and paste to reorder text and the find and replace function to make changes. Remind them they can also correct their work by using the delete and the backspace keys. Remind the children to save a copy of their letters as they will need them for the next lesson.

Ask the children to print out their letters and have them checked for spelling and grammatical errors by another pair.

Plenary

Project some of the children's letters on to the whiteboard. Pick out good use of organisational features such as paragraphs, bullet points and use of bold type in limitation, to ensure the letter is clear and well presented. Use the spelling and grammatical check to highlight any errors. Praise the children for error-free work.

Ask the other children to make suggestions for improvement and allow time for them to modify their letters in the light of these comments.

Extension

Split the children into small groups and ask them to write a reply to Josie's letter as if they were the local MP. Use hot seating and other drama techniques to encourage the children to write in the role of the MP. When they have drafted their letters they could type up their replies in Word and display them in the classroom.

Activity Four – Email

"How to use email to send and receive messages and compare this to other methods of communication."

Resources
- 'It's Not Right!' letter
- 'Communication' activity sheet
- PowerPoint presentations
- Computers
- Printer
- Digital projector
- Whiteboard
- Laptop
- Class email address.

Introduction

Using emails can help children to develop their reading and writing skills and develop their knowledge of the wider community. Before you undertake this activity it would be wise to get in touch with your local newspaper, county council or MP first and explain that you are doing a school ICT project involving the local environment. It is also important to ensure that the software you use is compatible with your target audience so that the attachments can be read. You may also like to ask if the recipient would kindly write a reply to the class acknowledging their work.

Read the 'It's Not Right!' letter to the class. Ask the children if they think emailing a letter in this way is a good idea. What will it achieve? Discuss with the class ways of sending messages over distances such as by letter, radio, telephone, etc. Describe some earlier methods of communication such as signalling flags, bonfires and Morse code. Ask the class to think about the advantages and disadvantages of these methods such as speed, confidentiality and permanence. Ask them to list their ideas on the Communication activity sheet.

Explain to the children they are going to email one of the letters and PowerPoint presentations to the local newspaper, county council or MP to let them know about the condition the area is in. If writing to your MP, tell them a little bit about the MP and their policies. It is also good practice to find a named person to write to when using local newspapers or the county council. This will make the recipient feel less anonymous and give the children an audience to write to.

Tell the children the presentation will be sent as an attachment. Discuss why correct spelling is important and explain that before a book is printed editors and proof-readers correct spelling mistakes.

Main Activity

Before the lesson begins add the recipient's contact email address to the school address book on the email facility used. Explain the address ensures that the email is received by the right person. Demonstrate to the class how to find the address by selecting it from the address book.

Have a competition in the class to choose the best letter and presentation to send. Explain to the class you can not send all of them as this will be like Spam/Junk mail. Tell them it is better to send one to represent their views. Remember to use a class email address to do this rather than an individual one.

Ask for a volunteer to copy and paste the letter they wrote as a Word document into the body of the email. Stress the importance of good spelling and presentation. Show them how to attach the chosen PowerPoint presentation to the email. It is important to explain to the children that different messaging programs attach file in different ways but, an attachment is usually indicated by the paperclip icon. Remind the children that attachments will not be able to be read by machines with incompatible software.

Show them how the attached file should appear in the 'attached' box. Point out the 'Send' button. When you are happy they understand, ask for a volunteer to send their email. You may wish to add a read receipt to show the children the person you are writing to has received it.

Plenary

Explain to the class sending an email is instant. It should only take a few seconds to arrive. If you send a message and it doesn't get returned to you or bounces back you can be sure it has arrived at its destination safely. Demonstrate how to check the Inbox or Junk mail facility for any emails that have been returned.

Extension

Ask the children to explain how they would reply to an email. Discuss the differences between the Reply, Reply to all and Forward functions in the email program used at school.

It's Not Right!

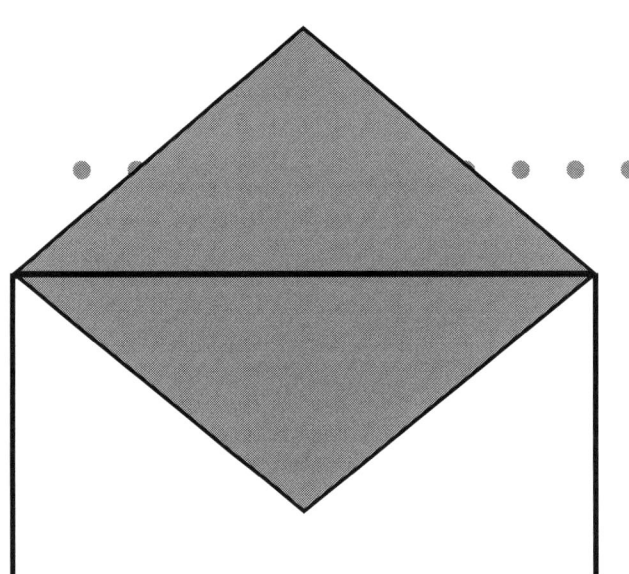

                                            Josie Fitzgerald,
                                            Anytown School,
                                                    Anytown,
                                            Yorkshire Dales

Dear Tim Farron MP,

I am writing to inform you about how dangerous my journey to and from school is with the hope that you can help to make changes that will improve the local area.

One of the main issues is that the trees and bushes along the public footpath are full of litter and weeds. The trees are also too tall and need cutting back. They block the light and make the footpath dark during the day. The branches of the trees and hedges are so big that in some places pedestrians have to walk single-file and we are in danger of having our eyes scratched out or being stung by the giant stinging nettles.

The council should provide more regular maintenance to ensure the pavements are kept clear especially in the alleyways on the way to school.

Using stories to teach **ICT** *Ages 7-9*

The footpaths are full of bushes, stinging nettles and dog mess on the ground. Why do dog owners allow their dogs to foul the footpaths and the local park area on the way to school? I think there should be more signs telling the dog owners to clean up after their pets. It should stress the risk of diseases to the children.

Dog mess can easily get spread across the pavement by pram and bicycle wheels. As well as being unsightly, it is unpleasant to smell and very difficult to remove from shoes and clothing. If somebody does tread in the dog mess, it can easily be trailed all the way through the school and into the classrooms.

If more bins were provided there would be no excuse for not being able to dispose of dogs' waste. Maybe, CCTV cameras could be erected to catch the regular offenders so that they can be issued a fine.

Another problem is the vandalism on the way to school. Many of the wooden panelled fences have been kicked in. Those that are remaining have rude words written on them. It also looks like someone has vandalised the low walls around the houses near the school.

The area directly outside the school is hazardous too. There should be double yellow lines in the road leading up to the school as the cars parking there create chaos for vehicles coming in and out of the school at the start and finish of the school day. It is dangerous for children, especially as it leaves nowhere to cross the road except in between the parked cars.

Some of the cars park on the pavement, which means we have to walk in the road to pass. Often there are cars parked in front of the dropped curb, which makes it very difficult to get pushchairs on and off the pavement. Some of the curb stones have also been broken by the cars tyres running over them. They need repairing as they are crumbly and treacherous.

Other cars park on the grass verges. In the wet weather, the tyres get stuck and spray mud on to the pavement. It makes it very difficult to pass without getting mud on our shoes. This mud gets all over the carpet in the classrooms. Sometimes, it is difficult to tell the difference between the mud and the dog mess.

I think the solution is to have a no tolerance policing policy where the police and traffic wardens give tickets to offenders parking in the wrong place outside the school entrance.

We live in a beautiful neighbourhood and it is being destroyed by vandalism, unkempt trees and bushes, dog fouling the pavements and car owners parking irresponsibly. You and the council need to do something about this.

Yours sincerely,

Josie Fitzgerald
Age 9
Yorkshire Dales

Local Visit

Name: _____

- List the things you like about the area you are visiting and the things you do not like.

Good points	Bad points

- Is there evidence of vandalism?

_____
_____
_____
_____

- Take some photographs to demonstrate what you found.

It's Not Right!

Name: _____

- Use this framework to plan your PowerPoint presentation.

Issue:		
Background information:		
Point of view	Facts	Evidence
Conclusion:		

Using stories to teach **ICT** *Ages 7-9*

Letter

Name: _____

- Write a draft of your letter outlining why you think the local area should be improved.

Letter

Communication

Name: _____

- List some different methods of communication.
  What are their advantages and disadvantages.

Method of communication	Advantages	Disadvantages

- Which methods of communication do you use most often?

_____

_____

- Why?

_____

_____

Using stories to teach **ICT** *Ages 7-9*

Mosaic – teachers' notes

Learning Objective
To develop visual ideas and to realise these ideas using ICT

Curriculum Links
Art

- Combine art forms imaginatively and in complementary and enhancing ways
- Understand that ICT can be used as an art medium in itself
- Use ICT to make images.

History

- Explore different ways we can find out about the past and how to understand the evidence
- Gain a knowledge of how communities, cultures and traditions have changed and are changing over time
- Enhance historical understanding by investigating myths and legends.

Activity One – Mosaic Design

"How to use a computer graphic package to develop an image."

"If you can use the 'fill' and 'save' functions of a computer graphic package."

Resources

- 'Mosaic' story
- 'Mosaic Design' activity sheet
- Computers
- Printer
- Digital projector
- Whiteboard
- Laptop
- Image search engine
- Graphic software such as Paint.

Introduction

Read the 'Mosaic' story to the class. Ask the children where Christina, Daniel and Joseph were? What were they looking at? What happened to them?

Ask if they have ever seen any mosaics? Look at some Greek and Roman mosaics on the Internet, as examples. Project the images on the whiteboard. Talk about how the images are made. Point out where the patterns on the mosaics are made of simple shapes and where they are based on animals, plants or other objects. What do the pictures tell us of Greek or Roman life? Tell the children they are going to design their own pictures to make a mosaic design, using the squares on the 'Mosaic Design' activity sheet.

They can design their own images of anything they like. They may get ideas from the images they have seen on the mosaic examples they looked at. Focus their art work by suggesting they choose something, from the story, like a bird, butterfly, sun, fountain, musical instrument, the island of Cyprus, etc.

Allow time for the children to draw and colour their mosaic designs on the activity sheet. Tell them to colour whole squares as much as possible to produce their designs.

Main Activity

Make a 20x20 square grid in Word and copy it into a graphic program such as Paint. Tell the children ICT can be used to create images. Ask the children to transfer their mosaic designs from the activity sheet onto the 20x20 grid on the screen. Explain they can do this by choosing the 'fill' icon and filling each square with the desired colour in the same way as they did on the 'Mosaic Design' activity sheet. All the children should recreate their pattern using the different medium. If some children have used half squares show them how they can draw a line with the pencil tool and fill the desired space. Remind them they must ensure there are no gaps in the lines, or the colour will leak out.

Tell the children if they click fill on the grid lines it will change the colour of the grid lines. When they have finished filling each square suggest they turn the grid lines white. This will give the impression of cement.

Remind the children to save their work as they go along. Explain their screen image is their finished product.

Plenary

Explain ICT can be used as an art medium in itself. Ask:

- In what ways does ICT help us to create images?
- What is harder to achieve with ICT than other media?

Extension

Children's work could be incorporated into an electronic 'art gallery' which could be added to the class page on the school website. This will encourage the children to see the version on the screen as the final one.

Activity Two – Andy Warhol

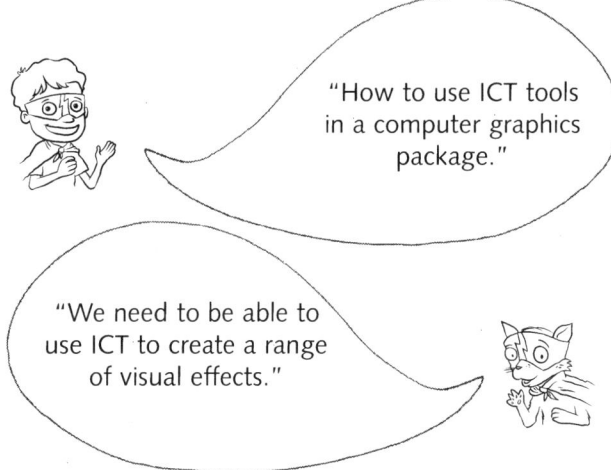

"How to use ICT tools in a computer graphics package."

"We need to be able to use ICT to create a range of visual effects."

Resources
- 'Mosaic' story
- 'Andy Warhol' activity sheet
- Computers
- Printer
- Digital projector
- Whiteboard
- Laptop

- Pictures of Andy Warhol's artwork, particularly the Campbell's Soup Can, Mickey Mouse and Marilyn pictures
- Art books and encyclopaedias containing information about Andy Warhol
- Search engine
- Graphic software such as Paint.

Introduction

Read the 'Mosaic' story to the children. Remind children that ICT can be used to develop images. Display the children's mosaic designs to the class by projecting them onto the whiteboard. Remind the class how ICT features such as cut, copy and paste can help them with their writing. Explain that they are going to use ICT to develop pictures, using similar tools and techniques.

Display a selection of pictures of Andy Warhol's artworks. Discuss the artwork's subject matter. Ask the children why they think Warhol chose to base so many of his artworks on famous identities and well-known yet everyday products like the famous Campbell's Soup Can. Discuss the use of repetition and colour in Warhol's work. Explain that Warhol was part of an art movement called 'Pop Art.' Ask the children where the term might have come from and how it would relate to Warhol's work.

Split the class into pairs. Using the 'Andy Warhol' activity sheet give the children fifteen minutes to find out everything they can about Andy Warhol using books, encyclopaedias, and the Internet. Ask them to make notes on the activity sheet as they research. Ask each pair to share with the class one fact that they have found out about the artist.

Main Activity

Project an image of Andy Warhol's Campbell's Soup Can picture on the whiteboard. Tell the children they are going to use their mosaic designs to make a similar repeating pattern by using their previously saved mosaic design.

Ask the children to locate their saved mosaic design. Explain they can cut this original design and paste it into a new document. This can then be resized and copied and pasted to produce images similar to Warhol's Campbell's Soup Can picture. Show the children how they can change the paper orientation to landscape using the page set up option on the file tab. Suggest they can experiment with the colours and backgrounds in their own pictures, as Andy Warhol did for his *Mickey Mouse* and *Marilyn* artworks.

Ask the children to save their drafts with different document names using the 'Save as' command to show the development of their design.

Plenary

Discuss how ICT helped them to create their designs. Print out some examples of draft and final patterns and compare them. Ask the children to talk about the changes they made to their work in progress.

Extension

If time permits children could use the digital cameras to take photographs of each others faces and to develop Andy Warhol pictures using his 'Marilyn' as inspiration. The pictures should be taken in front of a plain, light background for best effect.

Activity Three – Symmetrical Patterns

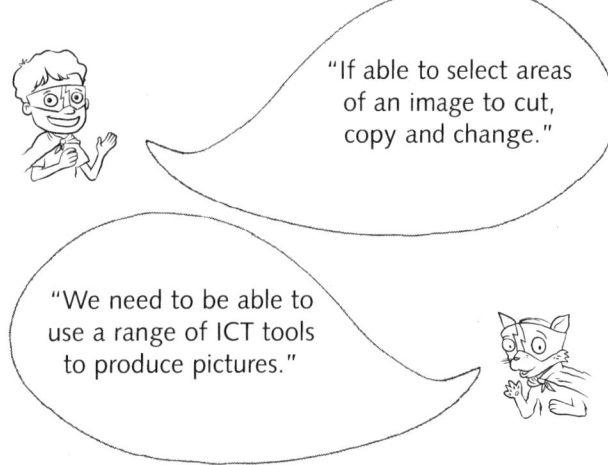

"If able to select areas of an image to cut, copy and change."

"We need to be able to use a range of ICT tools to produce pictures."

Resources

- 'Mosaic' story
- 'Symmetrical Patterns' activity sheet
- Computers
- Printer
- Digital projector
- Whiteboard
- Laptop
- Search engine
- Graphic software such as Paint.

Introduction

Read the 'Mosaic' story to the class. Remind children that ICT can be used to develop images. Display the children's mosaic designs to the class by projecting them onto the whiteboard. Remind the class how ICT features, such as 'copy and paste', can help them with their writing. Explain that they are going to use ICT to develop pictures, using similar tools and techniques. Demonstrate how areas of their designs can be selected copied and re-sized.

Tell the children they are going to use a range of visual effects such as reflection and symmetry to produce some interesting kaleidoscope effects with their own samples. Look at a selection of images that demonstrate symmetry. Some appropriate images for discussion can be found by doing a Google image search. Discuss how the pictures use symmetry. Point out patterns that have two axis of symmetry.

Show the children how a Paint program can create symmetrical patterns automatically.

Main Activity

Ask the children to select appropriate areas of their mosaic designs and copy and resize them. Ask the children to use these areas to create patterns using the symmetry tool. Encourage the children to recognise reflective symmetry in their design.

Tell the children to use fill to the background, trying different colours. Remind them to save their work regularly and if they use the 'Save as' function they can keep different versions of their designs.

Ask the children to print out a copy of their design on a white background to save ink and stick it onto the 'Symmetrical Patterns' activity sheet. Then, using a ruler and marker pen, ask them to add the lines of symmetry.

Plenary

Project on the whiteboard some examples of draft and final patterns and compare them. Ask the children to talk about the changes they have made to their work. Compare how they made their patterns on the computer using different types of media. Which effects are easier to produce with ICT? Which would be harder to produce?

Extension

Ask the children to print out multiple copies of their work and use the print outs, together with other collected images from magazines and those they have drawn, painted, made with chalks and pastels, etc. to make a mixed media collage.

Activity Four – Encyclopaedia

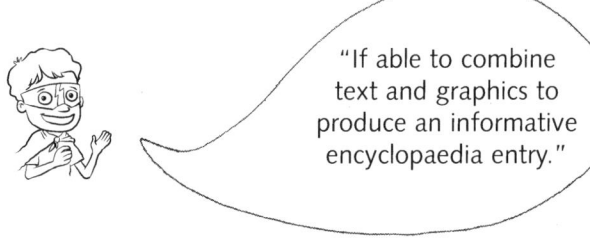

"If able to combine text and graphics to produce an informative encyclopaedia entry."

Resources
- 'Mosaic' story
- 'Encyclopaedia' activity sheet
- Computers
- Printer
- Digital projector
- Whiteboard
- Laptop
- Search engine
- Class book.

Introduction

Read the 'Mosaic' story to the class. Ask them what creature did Joseph and Daniel help to defeat. Explain this creature is from Greek mythology. Who do they think Aphrodite is? Could she be the goddess? Why or why not? What other mythical gods, goddesses and creatures do they know about?

Explain they are going to find out about Greek mythology to make an encyclopaedia about the Greeks. Tell the children encyclopaedias are organised in alphabetical order so that the entries are easier to find. Explain each entry will have a few sentences explaining a bit about them and a picture.
Use the list of mythological characters on the 'Encyclopaedia' activity sheet to help ensure that you have an entry with as many different letters of the alphabet as possible and that there are lots of different entries submitted. You could photocopy the activity sheet and cut out the names and let the children pick one form a hat. When they have completed that one, they could then choose another.

Main Activity

Allow time for the children to research their allocated Greek mythological character. Remind them they should write the information they find in their own words and not just copy and paste.

Suggest they choose an appropriate image to support their writing or they design their own in a graphics program.

Plenary

Print and stick their entries into a class made book. Keep the book on the class bookshelves and encourage the children to look at it during quiet and shared reading times.

Extension

It is possible to produce your own digital encyclopaedia in Word using hyperlinks. Create an encyclopaedia folder and an index page. Each entry should be written on a new page and saved with the character name as listed in the index. Each entry should link back to the index.

Using stories to teach **ICT** *Ages 7-9*

Mosaic

The heat was stifling. Mum and Dad had dragged us out to see the Ancient Greek mosaics. It wasn't the smartest idea they had ever had but, Mum is into history, mythology and stuff. She had been going on about the mosaics ever since we arrived in Cyprus last week. We had seen mosaics of musicians, birds, butterflies, gods and goddesses, deer, fish and now they were admiring an old, battered, Greek mosaic of a fountain.

I yawned. My brothers, Daniel and Joseph, scuffed their feet in the sand. Clouds of dust billowed into the air.

"Don't do that, boys," Mum scolded. "Dust might go in your eyes."

Daniel scowled. He shoved his hands deep into his short pockets. Joseph copied him.

"Why did we have to be here anyway?" Daniel moaned. "I'd rather be at the hotel. At least there's a swimming pool."

Mum and Dad were too engrossed in the mosaics to take any notice.

"Watch your brothers, Christina," Dad said, as they moved onto the next one.

I glanced at my brothers. Why did I always get stuck looking after them? Joe was grinning away to himself. He had found a bright green, plastic yo-yo in his pocket. He looped the string around his finger and tried a couple of the tricks Daniel had taught him.

"That's not how you do it?" Daniel said and tried to snatch the yo-yo away.

Joe screeched.

The yo-yo slipped from his finger and rolled across the dusty ground onto the mosaic. It stopped right in the middle of the fountain.

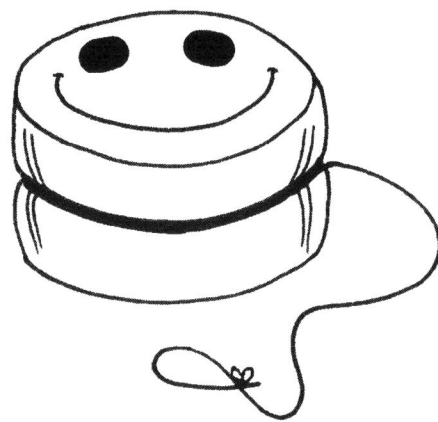

Joe immediately ducked under the rope.

"You're not allowed on there," I yelled after him.

He stood on the mosaic fountain, picked up the yo-yo, turned, smiled and vanished. Daniel gasped. "Where did he go?"

I shrugged, speechless.

We glanced at each other and both ducked under the rope in unison and ran onto the mosaic. We stood side by side on top of the fountain.

Suddenly, an amazing busy courtyard surrounded us. Daniel and I were stood by a real white marble fountain, exactly the same as the one shown in the mosaic. Water delicately trickled over the top bowl, into the middle bowl to be collected in the larger bowl at the bottom. People in white tunics wandered past. To one side of the fountain was a group of musicians. One played a flute and one played a stringed instrument that looked like a small harp. The music was soothing but, I could feel the panic rising in the pit of my stomach.

"Where could he have gone?" Daniel said. "We were right behind him."

"We have to find him," I said. "The last thing Mum and Dad told me to do was watch my brothers and I've lost one already."

A shrill scream startled us. Two white doves flapped frantically past, just missing my head. The musicians dropped their instruments and people ran in all directions. Daniel grabbed my hand and started to run, dragging me with him. Then I saw what everyone was running from - a giant Cyclops smashed into the wall at the far side of the courtyard. The small harp disintegrated under its enormous foot. Its single eye glowered as the Cyclops stomped towards us.

We ran out of the courtyard into a cobbled street. Whitewashed houses lined both sides. Sat on the doorstep of the furthest away house, was Joseph and a beautiful blond girl. He was showing her how to do a trick with his yo-yo. They were totally oblivious to the commotion created by the stampeding Cyclops.

We sprinted towards them.

"Where have you been?" I yelled at him.

But, there was no time to find out what had happened since he had disappeared. The Cyclops' giant fist smashed into the roof of one the houses. All that was left was a pile of rubble blocking our way. There was nowhere to go. We turned and faced the Cyclops.

"Cover your eyes," Daniel shouted. He kicked at the dirt sending up clouds of thick dust that swirled toward the Cyclops.

The Cyclops rubbed its eye as the dust cloud hit him. Tears streamed from both corners and down his cheeks. Joseph jumped up and stood on the top step. He shot the yo-yo forward, hitting the Cyclops right in the middle of his eye. The yo-yo sprung back. The Cyclops was blinded. There was a loud cheer and all the villagers rushed forward to bind the Cyclops legs. They tugged on the ropes and the Cyclops fell to the floor with a crash.

"Thank you," the little blond girl said. "We will make sure the Cyclops never terrifies the village again."

"This is my friend Aphrodite," Joseph said putting his yo-yo back in his pocket.

"Every few months the Cyclops comes to our village, stealing our food and destroying our homes," Aphrodite explained. "We are going to take if far away so it will not hurt anyone ever again."

My heart was still pounding but, the boys acted as if fighting Cyclops happened to them everyday of the week. We sat on the marble steps and listened to her stories about the Cyclops until it started to get dark. The sun began to set behind the houses casting a beautiful pink haze over the cobbled street. "It's time to go," I said and took Joseph's hand.

Joseph and Daniel waved goodbye to Aphrodite and we walked back towards the courtyard. When we arrived at the fountain we instantly reappeared where the mosaic was.

"Where did you get to?" Mum asked.

"You really shouldn't go wandering off," Dad said.

I stared at the mosaic of the fountain. "Look there is the wall the Cyclops smashed down," I said pointing to the left of the mosaic.

Daniel and Joseph rushed over to have a closer look.

"Have you seen the one of the Cyclops?" Dad asked. "It's over there."

We looked at each other and dashed to see it. The mosaics did not seem quite so boring after our adventure.

The End

Mosaic Design

Name: _____

- Design your own mosaic picture.

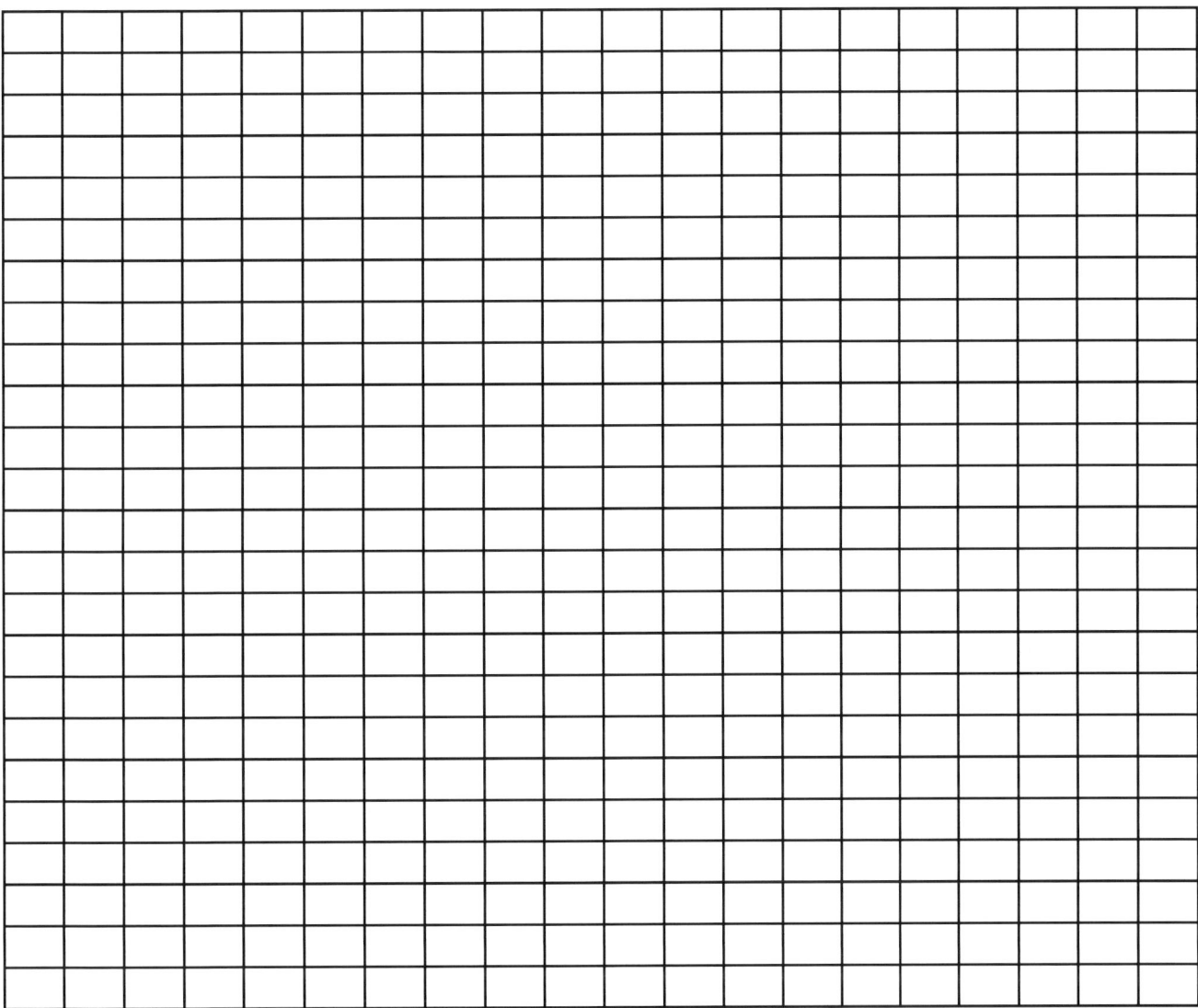

- Name your picture _____
- Recreate this picture on the computer.
- In what ways does ICT help us to create images?

_____

_____

_____

Using stories to teach **ICT** *Ages 7-9*

Andy Warhol

Name: _____

- What can you find out about Andy Warhol?

Artworks	Life

Influences	Other

- Write down your favourite fact about Andy Warhol

_____
_____
_____

Symmetrical Patterns

Name: _____

- Stick your symmetrical designs on to the activity sheet.
- Draw in the lines of symmetry.

- How many lines of symmetry did you find?

_____

Encyclopaedia

Name: _____

- Choose a Greek mythological character from the list below.

Achilles	Adonis	Amazons	Andromeda	Aphrodite	Apollo	Ares
Argonauts	Artemis	Athena	Atlas	Bacchus	Bellerophon	Centaurs
Chimera	Cronus	Cyclops	Daphne	Diomedes	Dionysus	Dryad
Echo	Electra	Eros	Fates	Golden Fleece	Gorgon	Hades
Harpies	Helen of Troy	Hercules	Hermes	Iris	Jason	Kraken
Laius	Laodamia	Laomedon	Midas	Minotaur	Morpheus	Muses
Narcissus	Nemesis	Nymphs	Odysseus	Oedipus	Orion	Orpheus
Pan	Pandora	Paris	Pegasus	Perseus	Poseidon	Prometheus
Psyche	Python	Rhea	Saturn	Sirens	Sphinx	Tantalus
Theseus	Titans	Triton	Unicorn	Uranus	Zephyrys	Zeus

- Use the Internet to find out some information about this character. List the websites you use.

_____
_____
_____

- Find an illustration to support your writing.

Labyrinth – teachers' notes

Learning Objective
- To explore simulations, explore options and to test their predictions
- To write a repeating procedure to produce a desired effect.

Curriculum Links
Mathematics

- Recognise and draw a range of polygons
- Identify the relationship between the number of sides on the finished shape and the required angle of turn
- Measure angles.

Activity One – Simulation

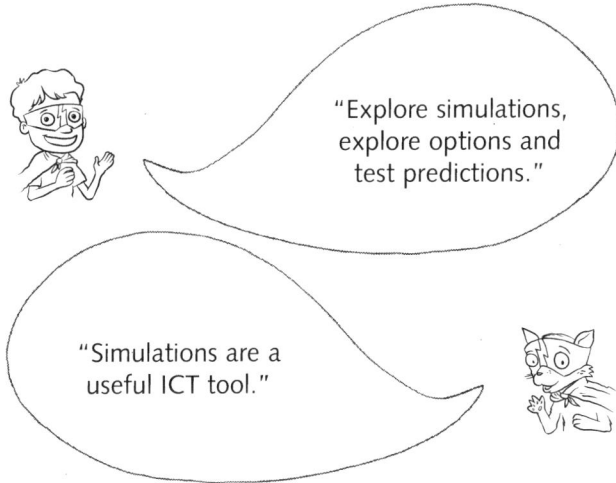

Resources
- 'Labyrinth' story
- 'Simulation' activity sheet
- Computers
- Printer
- Digital projector
- Whiteboard
- Laptop
- Simulation game such as Crystal Rainforest

Introduction

Read the 'Labyrinth' story to the class. Ask them if Leo designing a computer simulation to defeat the Troll was useful. Why or why not? Explain computer simulations can represent real or imaginary situations. Point out to the class simulations are usually simplified representations.

Tell the children computer simulations are used today to help people study and try ideas which would be difficult or impossible to do in practice. Simulations allow them to explore the different options. Ask the class to tell you some examples of where simulations would be useful, such as for training pilots, designing buildings and engine parts, testing products, etc.

What did Leo find was wrong with his simulation?

Main Activity

Explore the first part of a simulation in small groups. Give them a time limit. Ask them to record any decisions they made on the 'Simulation' activity sheet and the results of their actions. Bring the class together to share and discuss what they found out.

Ask the children to write down what they would like to do next when they use the simulation again. Encourage them to think of a variety of actions and write them down on the 'Simulation' activity sheet. Ask the children to choose one of their ideas to carry out and then record what happens.

Plenary

Discuss the changes that occurred in the simulation.

- How has it changed?
- What happens?
- Does it always happen?
- Is it a fair test?

Extension

Ask the children to identify any patterns in the simulation they have been using and ask them to suggest how they can test if these patterns are always true.

Using stories to teach ICT Ages 7-9

Activity Two – Evaluating Simulations

"If we can evaluate simulations end explain their usefulness."

Resources
- 'Labyrinth' story
- 'Evaluating Simulations' activity sheet
- Computers
- Printer
- Digital projector
- Whiteboard
- Laptop.

Introduction

Read the story to the class. Discuss what Leo found wrong with his simulation. How could he improve this?

Main activity

Load the simulation software on to the computers. Ask the children if they found any problems with the simulation they have been using?

Split the class into pairs. Read through the questions on the 'Evaluating Simulations' activity sheet.

- How is the simulation like/not like real life?
- What has been left out?
- Is it realistic?
- Is it helpful?
- Could it be improved?

Ask them to discuss these questions with their partner and note down their answers.

Plenary

Bring the class together and ask each of the questions in turn. List the children's ideas on the whiteboard. Encourage them to give reasons for their answers.

Extension

Ask the children to design their own idea for a simulation adventure game based on the labyrinth story.

Activity Three – Procedures

"To enter instructions to control a screen turtle."

"If able to write procedures to draw simple shapes."

Resources
- 'Labyrinth' story
- 'Procedures' activity sheet
- Computers
- Printer
- Digital projector
- Whiteboard
- Laptop
- Control software, such as Logo

Introduction

Read the story to the class. Ask the children if the commands Leo used remind them of anything they have used in school.

Show the children a control program where they have to write procedures to move a screen turtle, such as Logo. Discuss how they are similar and different to floor turtles. Tell them that the steps taken on the screen are smaller than the floor turtle steps.

Ask the children to predict what would be drawn if they enter the following sequence:

Repeat 360 [forward 1 right 1]

Ask them to test their predictions. Tell the children this is known as a procedure.

Ask them to predict what this sequence will draw:

Repeat 360 [forward 1 left 1]

Explain it will draw the circle but in the opposite direction.

Show the children how they can produce a dashed line by using the penup and the pendown commands.

Pendown
Forward 40
Penup
Forward 20
Pendown
Forward 40
Penup
Forward 20
Pendown
Forward 40
Penup

Explain they can also use this method to draw on different parts of the screen.

Main activity

Tell the children if they want to use a set of instructions over again, it is possible to give it a name. This is known as a procedure. The turtle will carry out all the instructions in the procedure when they type the procedure name. In this way, they can draw a series of the same shape:

Square
Forward 30
Square
Forward 30
Square

Split the class into pairs. Tell the children they are going to use the Logo software to investigate with their partner how to write procedures for the square, octagon and triangle by using the Repeat command. Give them each a copy of the 'Procedures' activity sheet. Give them time to experiment with the instructions to formulate their procedure. Tell them to give their procedures appropriate names and save them.

Tell the children when drawing a triangle, the turtle turns around the outside of each corner of the triangle.

Plenary

As a class check that each group have written their procedures correctly. The size of the shape may vary. Ask the children which number needs to be changed to make the shape smaller or bigger.

Procedure for drawing a square

Pendown
Repeat 3 [forward 50 right 90]
Forward 50
Penup

Procedure for drawing an octagon

Pendown
Repeat 7 [forward 50 left 45]
Forward 50
Penup

Procedure for drawing a triangle

Pendown
Repeat 2 [forward 50 right 120]
Forward 50
Penup

Using stories to teach ICT Ages 7-9

Extension

Once they have mastered drawing shapes and leaving spaces around them they will be able to use the computer to draw some lovely patterns. These can be printed out and displayed with the instructions and procedures for each shape.

Activity Four – Polygons

Resources
- 'Labyrinth' Story
- 'Polygon' activity sheet
- 'Space Exploration' activity sheet
- Computers
- Printer
- Digital projector
- Whiteboard
- Laptop
- Control software, such as Logo.

Introduction

Read the story to the class. Ask them what was the last shape they had to travel through when they were making their way through the labyrinth. Remind them it was a pentagon. Read the appropriate part of the story.

Before them appeared the last set of instructions:

'Repeat 5 [forward 100 right 72]'

"It's a procedure," Leo said and quickly programmed the Unicorn.

"Yes," Captain Jack said. "It's a procedure for a Pentagon. Each shape is going up by one side."

Ask the children what degree angle did he have to turn? Explain to the class that 72x5=360 and there are 360° in a circle. Ask the children to predict what will happen if they enter the following sequence into their logo type programs:

Repeat 5 [forward 100 right 360/5]

Ask them to test their hypothesis.

Main activity

Ask the children to use the 'Labyrinth' story and their knowledge of using the Repeat command to work out the instructions how to draw a Pentagon.

Split them into pairs and give them a copy of the 'Polygon' activity sheet. Ask the children to investigate how to draw the pentagon, hexagon and dodecagon and write the instructions and procedure on the 'Polygon' activity sheet.

Plenary

As a class, check each group have written their procedures correctly. The size of the shape may vary. Ask the children which number needs to be changed to make the shape smaller or bigger.

Ask the children to measure the angles of the shapes they have drawn, either on screen or on printouts. Are the angles the same even if the polygon is bigger or smaller?

Extension

Use the questions on the 'Space Exploration' activity sheet to encourage the children to find out more about space. Suggest they can present the information they find as a leaflet.

Labyrinth

Everything was quiet on the Spaceship Unicorn. Captain Jack was working with Leo on a simulation program. They were trying to calculate the best options to defeat their arch enemy, The Trolls. On the simulation Leo fired the ship's lasers and Ka-boom! The Trolls ship was blown to smithereens.

"No, No, No, No, No!" Captain Jack yelled.

"The Unicorn's graphics are not good enough," Leo complained. "The Trolls' ship is manoeuvring way too slow. I'm sure in real life it would easily turn about and shoot us first."

"It makes no difference if it doesn't meet our principal ruling," Captain Jack moaned. "We want zero casualties."

"Zero casualties…" Leo muttered under his breath.

Meanwhile, Zelda was in the lab. She was busy designing her new weapon – sleeping bombs. They were gold canisters filled with a special formulated gas to send their enemy to sleep. But, she was having difficulty getting the shiny gold cans to break. She did not want them to crack before they were ready to use them. But, each time she threw the sleeping bomb, it stayed intact, no matter how hard she threw it.

Suddenly there was a mighty bang and the Spaceship Unicorn shuddered.

Leo checked the monitors. "It's the Trolls."

There was another thunderous boom, as the Unicorn was hit by the Trolls' lasers again.

"Someone should explain the principal ruling to them," Leo moaned. "They don't seem to mind blowing us right out of the galaxy."

"Great!" Captain Jack said excitedly. "Now we can try the new lasers for real."

"But, we're not ready. I haven't adjusted them correctly to prevent their total annihilation. What about the principal ruling?"

"Reduce the lasers by fifty percent and target their engines," Captain Jack ordered. "We will leave them stranded."

"What's going on?" Zelda said, rushing into the control room still holding one of the sleeping bombs.

"The Trolls are attacking," Leo said, as he pressed the keys on the control panel, reducing the lasers by fifty percent. "Those pirates are probably after the amazing souvenirs we've collected during our adventures?"

Zelda said, as she went to her station. But, before she could reach her seat, she vanished. The Trolls had zapped her right off the Unicorn.

The Trolls' ship accelerated into hyper space and disappeared.

"Where have they gone?" Captain Jack yelled.

"I may be able to follow their vapour trail," Leo said.

"Do it quick!" Captain Jack slammed his fist down on the arm of the chair. "We must find Zelda."

Leo followed the vapour trail until he came to an abrupt halt. Straight ahead, the reflection of the Unicorn stared back at them. It was as though someone had hung a giant mirror in space.

"The trail stops here," Leo told Captain Jack.

"Fly around." Captain Jack ordered.

"We can't! Sensors show the mirror is surrounded by an elaborate system of force fields that would disintegrate the Unicorn if we touch them," Leo said.

"Open a communication channel," Captain Jack said calmly.

Leo opened the channel. The reflection of the Unicorn shimmered and words started to appear on the mirror.

> **'You must answer three questions to pass through the Labyrinth Zone.'**

The two space explorers waited and the words slowly changed to display the question:

> **'What is a Red Dwarf?'**

"Well that's easy," Captain Jack said. "Every Junior Space Cadet knows the answer to that."

Leo laughed. "Well the Trolls have never been known for their intelligence. Maybe this won't be as difficult as I thought."

Leo typed in the answer and pressed the Enter key. The writing before them changed:

> 'Forward 50, Right 120, Forward 50, Right 120, Forward 40.'

"It's a triangle," Captain Jack remarked.

Leo quickly programmed the Unicorn to manoeuvre through the labyrinth. The mirror slid back and they were able to move forward. One wrong move and they would be space dust. They mirror glided back into place behind them. There was no going back.

Soon they were confronted by another mirror, blocking their way. On it appeared another question:

> 'What is a Blue Giant?'

"This is way too easy," Captain Jack said. "Have you ever felt like you are flying into a trap?"

"Too late to turn back now," Leo said. "Each question we answer will take us one step further towards finding Zelda." Leo typed in the answer and the next set of instructions flashed up.

> 'Forward 50, Right 90, Forward 50, Right 90, Forward 50, Right 90, Forward 40.'

"Interesting," Captain Jack said. "Now we have a square."

Leo programmed the Unicorn and as soon as the mirror slid back, the spaceship continued its journey through the labyrinth until it reached the next mirror. The last question stood glimmering in front of them:

> 'What happens when a star goes Super Nova?"

Leo typed the answer. "You don't think they are leading us into a black hole do you?" he asked.

Using stories to teach ICT Ages 7-9

"No," Captain Jack replied. "They will not be able to get our treasure if we're sucked into a black hole."

Before them appeared the last set of instructions:

```
'Repeat 5
[forward 100 right 72]'
```

"It's a procedure," Leo said and quickly programmed the Unicorn.

"Yes," Captain Jack said. "It's a procedure for a Pentagon. Each shape is going up by one side."

The mirror slid back and the Unicorn slowly moved forward through the final stage of the labyrinth zone. In front of them lay the Troll's Lair. Leo landed the ship and they rushed out onto a silver platform. To one side there was a control panel and to the other a pile of metal pipe but, there was no where to go except into a bubbling purple ocean ahead.

Captain Jack put a piece of the metal pipe into the ocean and the bubbles dissolved it.

"It's an acidic ocean," he said.

"Captain Jack, Leo! Is that you?" Zelda's voice called from above.

They looked up to see Zelda suspended in a cage above the acidic ocean.

"Be careful it's a trap…" But, before Zelda could finish her sentence, three Trolls materialised in front of them.

"Give us the treasure," Scarab, the Chief Troll, growled.

At that moment a gold canister flew from Zelda's cage, landed on the platform and rolled towards them. It stopped at Scarab's feet.

"What's this?" Ruby, the female Troll asked. "Don't touch that," Captain Jack said. "It belongs to us."

Immediately Ruby picked up the gold can.

"Treasure," Krutal, the third Troll roared and snatched the can out of Ruby's hand.

Both Captain Jack and Leo took two steps backwards.

"Don't open that," Captain Jack said, "or you'll be sorry."

The three Trolls laughed. Krutal tried to crack the canister by smashing it hard with a metal pipe. Nothing happened. Leo and Captain Jack covered their mouth and noses with their hands and took another two steps back towards the Unicorn. Krutal hit it again. The sleeping bomb cracked and the red gas seeped out. Krutal dropped the can and fell to the floor.

Ruby cackled and picked the can up. "Is it perfume?" she asked sniffing at the red gas.

Ruby instantly collapsed on top of Krutal. "What have you done to them?" Scarab growled. "The treasure will be all mine!" He rushed into the red cloud of gas to get the gold can. Soon he was asleep too.

"Get me down from here," Zelda called to them.

Leo went to the control panel. "I can't! There's some sort of password," he said.

"Try 'Hexagon'," Captain Jack said.

Leo typed in the word 'Hexagon'. There was a crackle and a hiss. All the force fields in

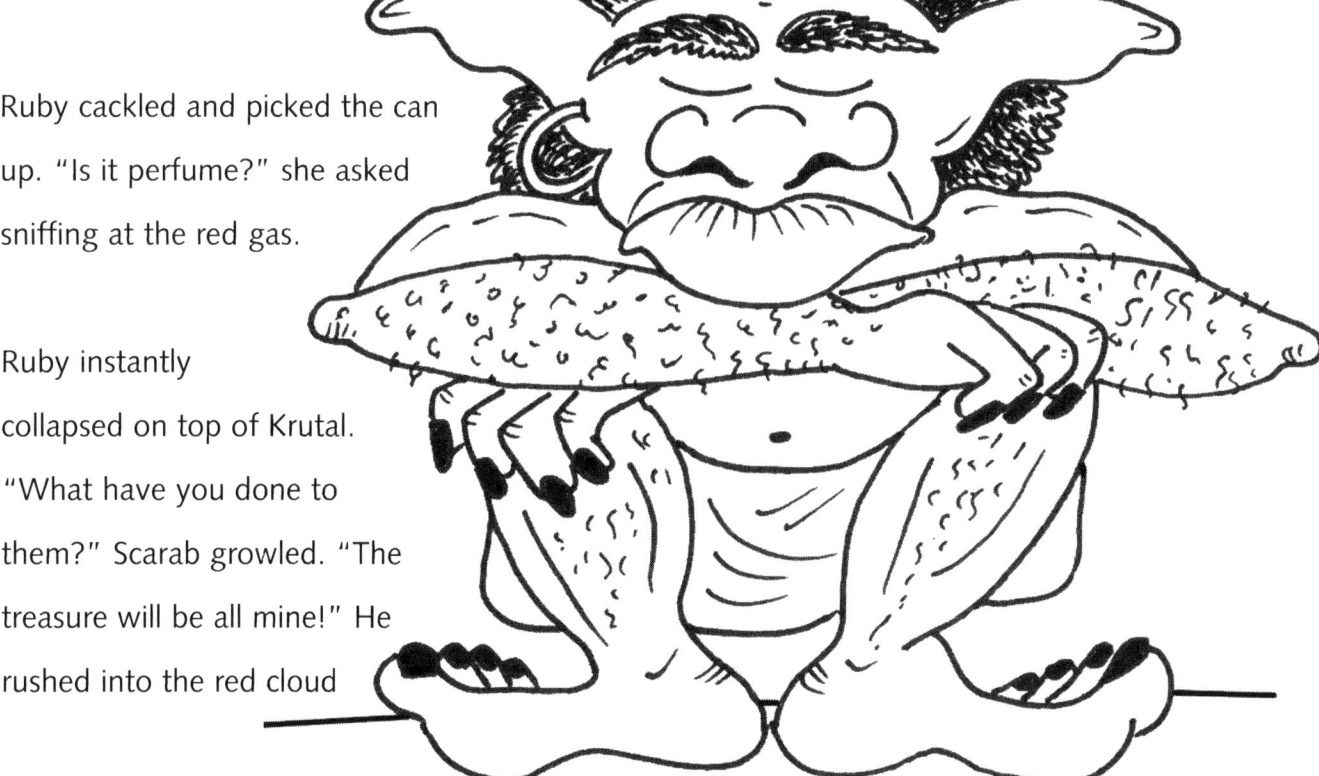

the labyrinth outside went offline. The cage lowered to the platform and Zelda climbed out.

"How did you know that?" she asked Captain Jack.

"It was the next shape in line," he replied.

Leo grinned. "At least we don't have to navigate the labyrinth zone again to get home," he said.

Zelda looked puzzled.

"Let's go," Captain Jack ordered, "before the Trolls wake up."

They left the three Trolls snoring. Soon they were zooming back through space on another adventure.

The End

Simulation

Name: _____

- Record the decisions you made during the simulation.
- What were the results of these actions?

Decision	Result

- What would you like to do next?

1 _____
_____

2 _____
_____

3 _____
_____

Simulation Evaluation

Name: _____

- Discuss the questions with your working partner.
- Note down your answers.
- Give reasons and examples for why you think this.

1. How is the simulation like/not like real life?

   _____
   _____

2. What has been left out of the simulation?

   _____
   _____

3. Is the simulation realistic?

   _____
   _____

4. Is the simulation helpful?

   _____
   _____

5. Could the simulation be improved?

   _____
   _____

Procedures

Name: _____

- Write the procedure for each shape, using the Repeat command.

Shape	Instructions	Procedure
Square	Pendown Forward 50 Right 90 Forward 50 Right 90 Forward 50 Right 90 Forward 50 Penup	
Octagon	Pendown Forward 50 Right 45 Forward 50 Right 45 Forward 50 Right 45 Forward 50 Right 45 Forward 50 Right 45 Forward 50 Right 45 Forward 50 Right 45 Forward 50 Penup	
Triangle	Pendown Forward 50 Right 120 Forward 50 Right 120 Forward 50 Right 120 Penup	

- What do you notice about these procedures?

_____
_____
_____

Polygons

Name: _____

- Write the instructions and the procedures for each of these polygons.

Shape	Instructions	Procedure
Pentagon (5 sides)		
Hexagon (7 sides)		
Dodecagon (12 sides)		

- What do you notice about these procedures?

_____

_____

Space Exploration

Name: _____

- Use the Internet to find out the answers to the following questions.
- Present the information you find in an interesting way.

- What is a Red Dwarf?

_____
_____
_____
_____
_____
_____

- What is a Blue Giant?

_____
_____
_____
_____
_____
_____

- What happens when a star goes Super Nova?

_____
_____
_____
_____
_____
_____